MINI
PARIS

YOUR TAILOR-MADE TRIP
STARTS HERE

Tailor-made trips and unique adventures crafted by local experts

HOW ROUGHGUIDES.COM/TRIPS WORKS

STEP 1
Pick your dream destination, tell us what you want and submit an enquiry.

STEP 2
Fill in a short form to tell your local expert about you dream trip and preferences

STEP 3
Our local expert will craft your tailor-made itinerary. You'll be able to tweak and refine it until you're completely satisfied.

STEP 4
Book online with ease, pac your bags and enjoy the trip! Our local expert will be on hand 24/7 while you're on the road.

PLAN AND BOOK YOUR TRIP AT
ROUGHGUIDES.COM/TRIPS

How to download your Free eBook

1. Visit **www.roughguides.com/free-ebook** or scan the **QR code** opposite

2. Enter the code **paris228**

3. Follow the simple step-by-step instructions

For troubleshooting contact: mail@roughguides.com

Contents

- **6** **Introduction**
  - 12 10 Things Not to Miss
  - 14 A Perfect Day in Paris
  - 16 Paris on a Budget
  - 18 Paris for Art Lovers
- **20** **History**
- **35** **Places**
  - 35 Île de la Cité
  - 42 Île St-Louis
  - 44 The Louvre, Tuileries & Concorde
  - 52 The Grands Boulevards
  - 55 Beaubourg, Les Halles & the Marais
  - 62 Bastille & Eastern Paris
  - 64 Champs-Élysées, Trocadéro & West
  - 71 Montmartre & Pigalle
  - 74 La Villette
  - 76 Latin Quarter & St-Germain-des-Prés
  - 84 Around the Eiffel Tower
  - 91 Montparnasse
  - 92 La Défense
  - 94 Excursions
- **99** **Things to Do**
- **110** **Food and Drink**
- **128** **Travel Essentials**
- **142** **Index**

Introduction

It's hard to argue with Victor Hugo's description of Paris as 'the city of cities'. For over two thousand years, it has steadily grown in size and reputation, and each of its many layers is rich in history and intrigue. Unlike many European cities, it was left almost unscathed by the two world wars, and its celebrated streets, monuments and museums still work their centuries-old magic today. And then there's the artistic heritage of the 'City of Light'; long a powerhouse of art, literature, music and philosophy. Little wonder then that Parisians are so proud to be part of a city that, according to writer Jean Giraudoux, has been home to, 'the greatest amount of thinking, talking and writing in the world'.

Geography

Paris centres around the River Seine, whose flowing waters have long been the lifeblood of the city. The River Seine enters Paris close to the Bois de Vincennes in the southeast and meanders gently north and south past three small, heavily developed islands – the Île St-Louis, Île de la Cité and, on its way out, Île des Cygnes.

WHEN TO GO

If you want great weather and you don't mind excess crowds, which can impact on the visibility of real local culture, then summer in Paris is for you, when the days are bright and the temperatures are warm. Paris in winter can be cold and grey, but it isn't as unappealing as it might sound. In fact, it can be quite cosy and romantic. Better still, there are great deals to be had on hotels and airfares.

On balance, spring and autumn are great times to visit Paris. During the spring months, sunny days are the rule rather than the exception, and in autumn, the occasional grey skies and showers tinge the city with a bit more gloomy romance.

The city has a fantastic café culture

Chains of hillocks add perspective to the city, with Montmartre (the city's highest point), Ménilmontant, Belleville and the Buttes Chaumont rising up to the north of the river, and to the south, Montsouris, the Mont Ste-Geneviève, Buttes aux Cailles and Maison Blanche. The city's compactness makes it very walkable and easy to explore, each quartier having a very distinct feel.

Government

At the beginning of the nineteenth century, Napoleon imposed a special status on the city of Paris, giving it the powers of a *département* in order to maintain a firm hold on the capital's politics and populace. Today, each *arrondissement* also has its own council and mayor to deal with local affairs. In the two houses of the French Parliament, 21 delegates and twelve senators represent the city.

WHAT'S NEW

The most noteworthy 'new' attraction in Paris is in fact rather old: the reborn Notre-Dame Cathedral, which reopened in December 2025 having been closed for five years after extensive fire damage.

A major artistic exhibition, the Met au Louvre, is running until September 2025, showcasing major pieces borrowed from New York's Metropolitan Museum, including artefacts from ancient Iran and Syria.

Elsewhere in the artistic world, the Centre Pompidou is undergoing renovations between late 2025 and 2030, with its collections relocated to a new building at 6 Av. du Maréchal Koenig, in the southern suburb of Massy. Other cultural openings in recent years include the Maison Gainsbourg (www.maisongainsbourg.fr/en), former home of controversial singer Serge Gainsbourg.

The luxury hotel scene is also anticipating a shake-up in the near future, with the opening of Louis Vuitton's first ever hotel in 2026.

The River

Fluctuat nec mergitur ('[She] is tossed by the waves but does not sink'), reads the Latin inscription on the capital's coat-of-arms, symbolising a city born beside the River Seine. Today, the Seine cuts a swathe through the city's middle and is the capital's widest avenue, spanned by a total of 37 bridges, which provide some of the loveliest views of Paris.

The river is the city's calmest thoroughfare, notwithstanding the daily flow of tourist and commercial boat traffic. In the nineteenth century, the banks were encumbered with washhouses and watermills, and its waters heaved with ships from every corner of France. More difficult to imagine are the seven hundred Viking warships that sailed up the river to invade Paris in the ninth century. Today, barges and pleasure boats ply the river, some on their way to Burgundy via the St-Martin and St-Denis canals, which cut across the northeast of the city.

Paris Ambience

One of the most persistent images of Paris is of long avenues lined with chestnut and plane trees. Flowers and plants abound in a patchwork of immaculate, formal squares, parks and gardens. Divided up by two long ribbons of streets, one tracing a long line north to south (from boulevard de Strasbourg to boulevard St-Michel) and the other running from east to west (from rue du Faubourg-St-Antoine as far as La Défense), Paris is a mosaic of *quartiers* (quarters) or 'villages', each with a distinctive character. Chains of boulevards encircle the city centre, marking its medieval boundaries. Several streets contain the word *faubourg*, indicating that they were once part of the suburb outside the city wall.

The city's rooftops at sunrise

The most important, unofficial division in Paris is between the traditionally working-class east and the mostly bourgeois west. In general, the further east you go, the further left you will find yourself on the political spectrum but massive urban renewal projects at Bercy and the 'new' Left Bank: Paris Rive Gauche (see page 81) in the southeast are continually transforming the city.

Lifestyle

Paris is a densely populated city, and it's expensive. Parisians often complain of being trapped in a monotonous rat race, locally encapsulated by the saying *Métro-boulot-dodo* (commute, work, sleep). As a tourist, though, tackle it at a slower pace and you'll likely find that it lives up to its reputation as one of the best cities on earth for enjoying the good life. A typical day might involve strolling lazily along boulevards, lingering over lunch at a neighbourhood bistro, and passing the afternoon at world-class museums. After dark, there's a vibrant nightlife scene, from romantic dinners followed by a moonlit stroll to nights of bar hopping, *chanson*, jazz or cabaret.

SUSTAINABLE TRAVEL

As the namesake of the international Paris Agreement on climate action, it's no surprise that Paris has made great strides in recent decades on sustainability. Between 2004 and 2018, in fact, Paris saw a twenty percent reduction in greenhouse gas emissions. To help do your bit, get around by renting a bike using the Vélib bikeshare system (www.velib-metropole.fr) – cycle paths have increased fivefold in Paris in the last twenty years – and make use of pedestrianised areas like that of the Left Bank, opened in 2016.

When buying food or products from markets and shops, look out for the label 'Fabriqué à Paris', which indicates that the item has been produced by local artisans. There are also a number of eco-friendly hotels to choose from, such as the zero-carbon Eden Lodge (www.edenlodgeparis.net).

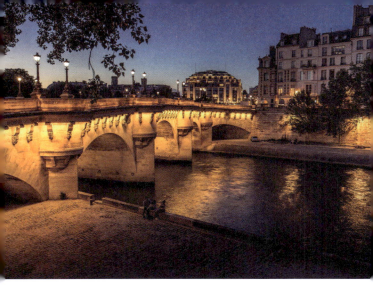

Pont-Neuf at night

CAFÉ CULTURE

Cafés have played a key part in the city's intellectual, political and artistic development. Café Voltaire (1 place de l'Odéon) was where, in the eighteenth century, Voltaire used to meet fellow philosopher Diderot to discuss their Enlightenment theories. The nineteenth-century poets Verlaine and Mallarmé also conversed here, and in the 1920s the American writers Ernest Hemingway and F. Scott Fitzgerald extolled the café's 'sudden provincial quality'. Between the two world wars, other writers spent hours at their favourite tables in Le Procope (13 rue de l'Ancienne-Comédie), while the Existentialist writer and philosopher Jean-Paul Sartre and his lover Simone de Beauvoir consolidated the reputation of Les Deux Magots (6 place Saint-Germain-des-prés) in the 1950s.

10 Things Not to Miss

1 CENTRE POMPIDOU
The inside-out museum showcases art from 1905 to the present day. See page 56.

2 ARC DE TRIOMPHE
Built to celebrate Napoleon's victories, it dominates the Champs-Élysées. See page 66.

3 EIFFEL TOWER
Built for the 1889 World Fair, it is still the most potent symbol of Paris. See page 88.

4 THE MARAIS
Atmospheric streets, museums, trendy bars, and some of the city's finest architecture. See page 59.

5 JARDIN DU LUXEMBOURG
The perfect Parisian park. See page 83.

6 THE LOUVRE
Once the home of kings, now home to the world's most outstanding art collection. See page 45.

7 MONTMARTRE
Artistic heritage, lively bars and some of the most romantic streets in the city. See page 71.

8 PLACE DES VOSGES
One of Paris' most lovely squares. See page 61.

9 NOTRE-DAME
A monument to Catholicism and the skill of the great Gothic architects. See page 36.

10 MUSÉE D'ORSAY
A treasure trove of Impressionist works. See page 86.

A Perfect Day in Paris

8.00AM

Breakfast. If your hotel doesn't serve breakfast, ask the concierge for directions to the nearest good *boulangerie*; buy some freshly baked croissants or *pains au chocolat* and find a leafy square nearby to eat them in.

9.00AM

Seine boat tour. Make your way to the western tip of the Île de la Cité, via the steps down from Pont-Neuf. From here, take one of the Vedettes du Pont-Neuf boat tours; it is a lovely way to see the city.

10.30AM

Rue de Seine. From Pont-Neuf, walk along quai de Conti, then amble down characterful rue de Seine with its art and fashion boutiques.

11.00AM

Coffee break. At the Palais du Luxembourg, turn left and walk along the railings of the famous Jardin du Luxembourg, the most elegant of Paris's parks. Stop for a strong espresso at smart café *Le Rostand* (see page 126), on the square at the garden's eastern tip.

12 NOON

Park and lunch. After a stroll through the Jardin du Luxembourg among joggers, *boules* players and smooching couples, make your way to nearby restaurant *La Ferrandaise* (see page 126) and enjoy a light lunch of French classics.

2.00PM

Paris history. Walk towards the river along teeming boulevard St-Michel, then catch the Métro to St-Paul. Walk up rue Malher to the Musée Carnavalet (see page 60) and spend an hour or two exploring Paris's history through the paintings and artefacts.

4.30PM

Retail therapy. Make your way back to Métro St-Paul and go straight to Charles-de-Gaulle-Étoile station. Take a moment outside the station to admire the Arc de Triomphe (see page 66), then walk down the Champs-Élysées, dipping into the swanky, big-brand shops as you go.

6.00PM

Montmartre and dinner. Take the Métro to Abbess. Follow your nose through the atmospheric, winding streets. After a relaxed bistro dinner at *Chez Toinette* (see page 124), walk to Sacré-Cœur and savour the panoramic view over the city from its front steps.

9.30PM

Bar hopping. Walk downhill to boulevard de Rochechouart and take a taxi to the République and Oberkampf area, which is littered with trendy bars. Try rue Jean-Pierre Timbaud, which runs parallel to rue Oberkampf, just east of place de la République – the perfect counterpoint to the historic attractions you saw earlier.

Paris on a Budget

7.00AM

Sunrise at Sacré Cœur. Rise early and make the walk up to the top of Montmartre to experience sunrise at the Sacré Cœur, the city's second-most iconic church behind Notre Dame. Dusk is another beautiful time to visit, but tends to be very busy.

9.00AM

Breakfast. Begin the day with a light breakfast Parisian-style consisting of a coffee and a croissant at a neighbourhood café or boulangerie. Eating 'on the go' tends to be frowned upon in Paris, so pull up a chair and enjoy at your leisure.

10.00AM

Montmartre. Take a walking tour through Montmartre, home to bohemians and artists for centuries. A free walking tour departs from the Abbessess Metro station each morning (book at www.guruwalk.com) – bring some cash for a tip. You'll see the former home of Vincent Van Gogh, and restaurants where Picasso would pay his bill by sketching on receipts.

1.00PM

Lunch. Walk south from Montmartre and enjoy lunch at *Chartier*, a historic restaurant which combines a glamorous Belle Epoque interior with a surprisingly cheap menu. Options include bistro classics like roast chicken and fries, but you can also try something a bit different in the form of grilled pig's trotter or beef tongue.

3.00PM

The Louvre. Continue walking south until you reach the Louvre. This magnificent art museum is free on the first Sunday of the month, and is always free for children, meaning that it's not a bank-breaking attraction for families. Even if you don't go in, it's worth admiring its iconic façade and glass pyramid, before heading to the Tuileries Garden (free) for a stroll. This lovely landscaped garden was created in 1664 at the instigation of King Louis XIV.

5.00PM

Palace art. Continue to the banks of the Seine and make the short walk to another free attraction, the Petit Palais. This art museum, housed in a magnificent building built for the 1900 Exposition Universelle, offers free entry to its permanent exhibitions, which include works by the likes of Rembrandt, Moent and Cézanne.

7.00PM

The Marais. Jump on the Metro at Champs-Élysées-Clemenceau and ride east for seven stops to Saint-Paul, where you'll find one of the best budget eating options in Paris. *L'As du Fallafel* is a legendary Middle Eastern restaurant which has been serving falafel wraps, shawarmas and salad plates at great prices since 1979. The Saint-Paul area is a lovely village-like spot in the heart of the Marais – it's worth spending the rest of the evening here, with a handful of fun pubs and bars.

Paris for Art Lovers

8.00AM
The Louvre. Paris is one of the world's great art cities, and the Louvre is among the world's most famous museums – so get there early. It opens at 9am, but arrive at 8am to beat the worst of the crowds and get in line. Once inside, you'll agree it's worth the early start as you admire masterpieces by the likes of Leonardo da Vinci, Bellini and Caravaggio, as well as statuary from ancient Greece and Rome and Egyptian artefacts. Allow a couple of hours to explore.

11.00AM
The Tuilleries. A short walk from the Louvre are the gardens and former palace of the Tuileries, where you'll also find a couple of art galleries. The first is the Centre National de la Photographie, which showcases a wide range of photography. The second is the Musée de l'Orangerie, which exhibits eight of Claude Monet's famous paintings of water lilies. There are also works by the likes of Picasso and Renoir on display in the downstairs gallery.

1.00PM
Lunch. You'll be hungry by now, so drop in for lunch at Le Grand Véfour, a gorgeous restaurant around 10 minutes' walk from the Tuileries. It's a work of art in itself – dating from the 1700s, it has high mosaiced ceilings and a wonderful gilded interior. It has a menu to match, too, of refined classic brasserie dishes such as pan seared scallops and stewed pork loin.

3.00PM
Musée des Arts et Métiers. Walk northeast for half an hour or so (or get the Metro to Réaumur-Sébastopol) and visit the fantastic Musée des Arts et Métiers. Although this is a science museum and not an art gallery, its collections of antique clocks, steam engines and classic cars, and its setting in an elegant historic monastery, will scratch a certain aesthetic itch that the city's art institutions can't.

5.00PM
Musée Picasso. While you're in the Marais neighbourhood, make your final museum of the day the fantastic Musée Picasso, home to the world's largest collection of artworks by Pablo Picasso. The collection includes world-famous pieces like *Man with Guitar* and *Le Matador*, and was re-opened after renovations in 2024 to include a section dedicated to Françoise Gilot, Picasso's former muse and partner who was a superb painter in her own right.

7.00PM
Dinner. A ten-minute walk from the Musée Picasso is *Au Petit Fer à Cheval*, a gorgeous café-bar which dates back to 1903 and has long been a favourite with the city's artistic set. It's a tiny, bustling place, so squeeze onto one of the dark-wood tables, order a *carafe de vin* and enjoy some people-watching as you savour one of the excellent bistro dishes on offer – steak frites, duck confit, and the like.

History

Paris began as an island fishing community and trading port in the middle of the River Seine. Stone Age inhabitants left some of the earliest traces (4500BC) on the Right Bank under what is now Bercy, but it was c.250BC before the town took form under the skilful hands of the Parisii. According to the Greek geographer Strabo, the Celtic tribe built their main city on the largest island on the river, presumably the Île de la Cité. The island, well away from the banks of the river – much wider than today – may well have provided refuge from the fierce Belgae to the east. The Parisii minted their own finely crafted gold coins for trade as far afield as Britain and the Mediterranean, and the town's prosperity and strategic position attracted the attention of Julius Caesar, whose legions conquered it in 52BC.

Clovis, King of the Franks

According to some philologists, the town's Gallo-Roman name of Lutetia means 'marshland', reflecting the character of the land that then bordered the river. The Romans built their settlement just above the flood plain, on what is now the Left Bank's Latin Quarter. Rue St-Jacques and rue St-Martin follow the route of the old Roman road linking northern France to Orléans. Scant subterranean masonry has been found from the Roman buildings – forum, theatres, temples – but there are substantial remains of the public baths in what is now a wing of the Musée National du Moyen Age.

Huns and Franks overran Roman Gaul in the third century, driving the citizens to retrench in the fortified Île de la Cité, which was renamed Paris around this time. In 508, Clovis, King of the Franks, set up court here. He later converted to Christianity, and several religious foundations date from this time, including those of the city's oldest church, St-Germain-des-Prés.

> **NOTES**
>
> France has no official state religion, but the sway of the Catholic Church during the nation's long history is still very much in evidence. As well as its many Catholic churches, Paris has a long list of places of worship dedicated to other varieties of Christianity and other faiths, notably Judaism, Islam and Hinduism.

The Capetians

Norman pirates regularly raided Paris from AD 845 onwards. The city stagnated until 987, when Hugues Capet, Count of Paris, became King of France. His Capetian dynasty went on to make the city the economic and political capital of France. The River Seine was once again the key to commercial prosperity, symbolised by the ship on the city's coat-of-arms. The Right Bank port area, known as the Grève, developed around the site of the present-day Hôtel de Ville.

Philippe Auguste (1180–1223) used the revenue from trade to build the Louvre fortress (its lower ramparts are clearly visible beneath today's museum), Notre-Dame Cathedral, paved streets, aqueducts and freshwater fountains. To protect his investment while he was away on the Third Crusade, he surrounded the city with walls.

The profoundly devout, and later canonised, Louis IX (1226–70) gave the city one of its great Gothic masterpieces, Sainte-Chapelle. His patronage of spiritual and intellectual life also gave rise to the learned character of the modern-day Latin Quarter. The Sorbonne University evolved from the many new schools established here, frequented in their day by Latin-speaking clerics and established by the king's chaplain, Robert de Sorbon. By the end of Louis's reign, Paris was one of the largest cities in Western Christendom, with a population of 100,000.

In the fourteenth century, the city's merchant class took advantage of the political vacuum left by the devastating Black Death and the Hundred Years War with England. In 1356, with King Jean le Bon held prisoner at Poitiers, Etienne Marcel – the merchants' leader – set up a municipal government in Paris. Although he was assassinated two years later, he had shown that the Parisians were a force to be reckoned with.

English Rule and Religious Conflict

Civil unrest continued unabated. In 1407 – during the second phase of the Hundred Years War between England and France – the Duke of Burgundy had the Duke of Orléans assassinated on rue Barbette, which led to twelve years of strife between their supporters. The Burgundians allied themselves with the English, who entered Paris in 1420, following the French defeat at Agincourt under Henry V, the English King. Henry had just signed the Treaty of Troyes with King Charles VII of France, which made him Regent and his son, Henry VI, King of England and France, at nine months old. Charles VII retained vast territories in central and southern France and, ten years after Troyes, Joan of Arc was able to lead the French army to several important victories in France, while England was divided by its nobles' interests. The Treaty of Arras (1435) between Charles VII and Henry's former ally, Philip III of Burgundy, brought the dual monarchy to an end. Charles VII reclaimed Paris in 1436

Place des Vosges

and by 1453 the English Monarchy had lost all its possessions in France, save Calais.

In the early sixteenth century, Paris thrived under an absolutist and absent monarch, François I (1515–47), who was occupied with wars in Italy, and even imprisoned for a year in Spain. Much of the Louvre was torn down and rebuilt along the present lines. A new Hôtel de Ville (city hall) was begun, as well as the grand St-Eustache church.

The new splendour was soon bloodied by religious war, starting in 1572 with the St Bartholomew's Day massacre of three thousand Protestants in Paris and culminating in the siege of the city by Henri de Navarre in 1589. Before the Catholic League capitulated, 13,000 Parisians had died of starvation. Henri was crowned at Chartres and finally entered the capital in 1594 – not before having converted to Catholicism himself, though his quip, 'Paris is well worth a Mass' is almost certainly apocryphal.

Henri IV did Paris proud once he was its master. He built the beautiful place des Vosges and place Dauphine, embellished the banks of the river with the quai de l'Arsenal, quai de l'Horloge and quai des Orfèvres, and even constructed the Samaritaine hydraulic machine that pumped fresh water to Right Bank households until 1813.

During the reign of Louis XIII (1610–43), Paris began to take on the fashionable aspect that became its hallmark. Elegant houses sprang up along rue du Faubourg-St-Honoré, and the magnificent *hôtels* (mansions) of the nobility were constructed in the Marais. The capital strengthened its hold on the country with the founding of a royal printing press and Cardinal Richelieu's Académie Française.

Paris increasingly attracted nobles from the provinces – although too many for the liking of Louis XIV, *le Roi Soleil* ('the Sun King', 1643–1715). To bring his overly powerful and independent aristocrats into line, Louis decided to move the court out to Versailles, compelling the courtiers to live at ruinous expense in his enormous new palace.

Paris lost some of its political importance, but looked more impressive than ever, with the landscaping of the Jardin des Tuileries and the Champs-Élysées, and the building of the Louvre's great colonnade and the Invalides hospital for wounded soldiers. The city asserted a leading cultural position in Europe with its new academies of the arts, literature and sciences and the establishment of the Comédie Française (1680) and several other theatres.

The rumble of popular discontent grew louder however, as corruption and heavy taxes for costly foreign wars marked the reigns of the Sun King's successors, the languid Louis XV (1715–74) and the inept Louis XVI (1774–93). One of the final construction projects of the *ancien régime* was a 23km (14 mile) wall encircling the city. Begun in 1784, it was a key factor in the subsequent unrest, for at points along the wall taxes were collected on goods brought into the city.

The Revolution

Paris was the epicentre of the political earthquake that was the French Revolution, whose aftershocks spread across France to shake up a whole continent. It started with protests about taxes, but turned into an assault on the privileges of the monarchy, the aristocracy and the church. Middle-class intellectuals made common cause with the urban poor, the previously powerless *sans-culottes* (literally, people without breeches). The revolutionaries destroyed the prison-fortress of the Bastille on 14 July 1789, and proceeded to execute the perceived enemies of the new republic.

A climax was reached on 21 January 1793, with the public beheading of Louis XVI. In the Reign of Terror later that year, several revolutionaries followed Louis to the guillotine: Camille Desmoulins, the fiery orator; Danton, who tried to moderate the Terror; and then the men who had organised it, Robespierre and Saint-Just.

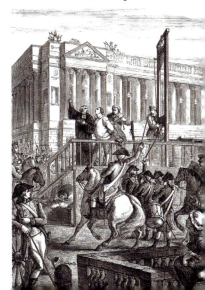

Louis XVI faces the guillotine

First Empire

In 1799, Napoleon Bonaparte became first consul, and later made himself emperor. For Paris, he performed all the functions of an enthusiastic mayor, scarcely hindered by his military expeditions abroad. Detailed maps of Paris and architectural plans for new buildings were always part of his baggage. For all his spectacular monuments – the Arc de Triomphe is one example – the emperor was proudest of his civic improvements: better fresh water supplies, improved drainage, new food markets and a streamlined municipal administration and police force. Most of his reforms survived long after his final defeat in 1815.

The Restoration

Although the monarchy was restored in 1814, it faced an ever-present threat in Paris from dissatisfied workers, radical intellectuals and a highly ambitious bourgeoisie. In July 1830 protest turned to riots and the building of barricades. Charles X was forced to abdicate. However, instead of restoring the republic, the revolutionary leaders played it safe and accepted the moderate Louis-Philippe, the so-called 'Citizen King'.

Napoleon Bonaparte

The Revolution of 1848, which brought Louis-Philippe's monarchy to an end, likewise started with riots and barricades in the streets of Paris. A mob threatened the royal palace, forcing the king to flee; they then invaded the Chamber of Deputies, demanding a republic. Elections followed, but they showed that however radical Paris might be, the rest of France was still largely conservative. The new National Assembly withdrew the concessions that had been made to the workers, and up went the barricades again. This time the army was called in with its heavy guns. At least 1,500 insurrectionists were killed, and thousands deported.

> **NOTES**
>
> Masonry from the Bastille was used to build the bridge leading to what was then the place de la Révolution – now place de la Concorde – where the guillotine was erected.

Second Empire

The democratically elected president, Louis-Napoleon (a nephew of Napoleon Bonaparte, whose son had died young), seized absolute power in 1851 and the following year became Emperor Napoleon III. Fear led him to modernise Paris. The insurrections of 1830 and 1848 had flared up in the densely populated working-class districts around the centre, and he wanted to prevent a recurrence. He commissioned Baron Georges Haussmann to do away with the narrow and insalubrious alleys that nurtured discontent, and moved the occupants to the suburbs. The city was opened up with broad avenues; these so-called *grands boulevards* were too wide for barricades and gave the artillery a clear line of fire in case of revolt.

The Second Empire was a time of joyous abandon and expansion, but the emperor stumbled into war against Prussia in 1870. The army was quickly defeated, and Napoleon III's disgrace and capture brought the proclamation of a new republic, followed by a crippling Prussian siege of Paris. The city held out, albeit reduced to starvation level. When France's leaders agreed to peace, there was another uprising.

Third and Fourth Republics

The Paris Commune, the surprisingly moderate and efficient rule of an elected revolutionary council, lasted ten weeks, from

General Charles de Gaulle

18 March to 29 May 1871, until Adolphe Thiers, the first president of the Third Republic, sent in troops from Versailles to crush it. In the last days, the *communards* set fire to the Palais des Tuileries and executed hostages. At least twenty thousand Commune supporters were executed in retaliation.

Prosperity rapidly returned, marked by a great construction boom. Projects begun under Napoleon III, such as the Palais-Garnier and the huge Les Halles market, were finished. The city showed off its new face at the 1889 World Fair, with the Eiffel Tower as its monumental centrepiece. The splendid Métro system was inaugurated in 1900.

After this period of peace, however, two wars took their toll. The Germans failed to take Paris during World War I, but occupied it for four years (1940–44) during World War II. The city escaped large-scale bombing, and Hitler's vengeful order to destroy the city before retreating was ignored. Liberation came eventually, with a grand parade down the Champs-Élysées by General Charles de Gaulle, his Free French forces and US and British allies.

The post-war city regained its cultural lustre under the influence of figures such as Camus, Sartre, Juliette Gréco and bebop musicians. Under a rapid succession of governments, however, economic recovery was slow.

Fifth Republic

The Fourth Republic collapsed in 1958 after an army revolt during the colonial war in Algeria. Recalled from retirement, de Gaulle became the first president of the Fifth Republic and set about the task of restoring French prestige and morale.

From the 1968 Riots to Mitterrand's Presidency

Barricades and insurrection hit Paris again in May 1968. With workers on strike, students hurled the Latin Quarter's paving stones at the Establishment. However, national elections showed that Paris was once more at odds with most of France, which voted for stability. Succeeding de Gaulle, Georges Pompidou affirmed the new prosperity with controversial riverside expressways and skyscrapers, and the striking Beaubourg cultural centre that bears his name.

In 1977 Jacques Chirac became the first democratically-elected mayor of Paris in over a century. Although many questioned his taste in approving the shopping mall that replaced the old markets of Les Halles, Chirac is credited with the effective clean-up of the formerly dirty streets.

President François Mitterrand (1981–95) made his mark on the Paris skyline with a series of imposing works (his *grands projets*):

FAMILY VALUES

France's birth rate of 2.01 children per family exceeds the European average, but is still a source of concern for the state. Every *famille nombreuse* (families with three children or more) is rewarded with benefits including nursery provision, subsidised public transport, car tax and school meals, as well as free admission to museums. The current population of France is around 68.2 million. The birth rate has been boosted by France's large Muslim community, whose numbers are, according to many demographers, steadily rising.

the pyramid centrepiece of the reorganised Louvre, the Grande Arche de La Défense, the Opéra Bastille, the Institut du Monde Arabe and the national library that bears his name.

Paris Today

Chirac became president in 1995. However, within two years his popularity had dwindled, and the Socialist leader Lionel Jospin became prime minister. Their period of joint stewardship was one of economic growth, reduced unemployment and rising property values. In 2001 Bertrand Delanoë became the city's first Socialist mayor for 130 years. Although Chirac beat the National Front candidate Jean-Marie Le Pen in the 2002 presidential election, the support for Le Pen was shocking. In his second term, President Chirac led a determined opposition to the war in Iraq, which saw his ratings soar, only to plummet after initiating reforms to the state pension and benefit system. His party's candidate to succeed him, Nicolas Sarkozy, won the presidency in May 2007 with promises of sweeping economic and social reforms. His 'Grand Paris' scheme, which aimed to make the city and its suburbs a single administrative unit, saw improved transport links and the construction of landmark skyscrapers. However, he alienated voters with his high-handed style and fondness for luxury; so much so that in 2012 François Hollande became the first Socialist president since François Mitterrand. In April 2014, Anne Hidalgo was elected the first female mayor.

In January 2015, twelve people were killed and eleven injured in an attack by the so-called Islamic State on the Paris headquarters of the satirical magazine, *Charlie Hebdo*. Following the attack, hundreds of thousands of people participated in marches against terrorism. However, terrorism also marred the end of the year, when Islamist extremists struck once again, killing 130 people and injuring hundreds more in a series of coordinated attacks across the city on 13 November. In the 2017 presidential election,

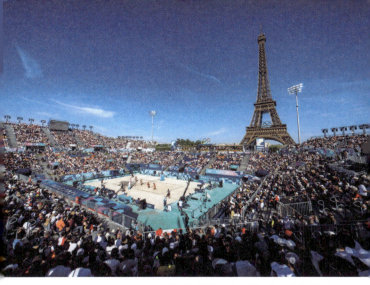

The Paris Olympics at the Stade Tour Eiffel

relative newcomer and leader of the En Marche! "radical centrist" party, Emmanuel Macron, swept to victory against Marine Le Pen's extreme far-right Front National and became the youngest head of state since Napoleon. Whether he can fulfil his promise to introduce radical economic reforms remains to be seen, but the political establishment has certainly been shaken up. The tentatively optimistic mood in France blossomed into full-blown joy when, in July 2018, it won the FIFA World Cup.

The 2020s began for Paris as for the rest of the world: in inauspicious style, with the coming of Covid-19, which plunged Paris into lockdown. In keeping with much of Europe, the following years saw a shift towards the political right in France, with Marine Le Pen's National Rally making major gains and Macron's Renaissance party significant losses in the 2024 legislative election.

Notre-Dame in flames in 2019

Chronology

c.250 BC Celtic settlement in the Paris area.
52 BC Roman conquest and founding of Lutetia on the Left Bank.
508 Clovis, King of the Franks, makes Paris his capital.
987 Hugues Capet elected King of France.
1431 Henry VI of England crowned King of France.
1436 English expelled.
1594 Henri IV enters Paris.
1682 Louis XIV moves court to Versailles.
1789 Storming of Bastille starts French Revolution.
1793 Execution of Louis XVI and Marie-Antoinette; Reign of Terror.
1804 Napoleon Bonaparte becomes emperor.
1814–15 Fall of Napoleon; restoration of Bourbon monarchy.
1848 Revolution brings Louis-Napoleon to power.

1870–1 Franco-Prussian War; Second Empire ends; Paris besieged.
1871 Paris Commune – 10 weeks of workers' rule.
1900 First Métro line opened.
1914–18 World War I. Germans advance to within eight miles of Paris.
1939 World War II begins.
1940 French government capitulates; Germans occupy Paris.
1944 Free French and other Allied forces liberate Paris.
1958 Fall of Fourth Republic. De Gaulle becomes president.
1968 Student riots, workers' general strikes.
1977 Jacques Chirac becomes first elected mayor since 1871.
1981 President Mitterrand elected president.
1995 Jacques Chirac elected president.
2002 The euro replaces the franc as France's unit of currency.
2007 Nicolas Sarkozy elected president.
2012 Socialist François Hollande elected president.
2014 Anne Hidalgo of the Socialist Party is elected Paris's first female mayor, with a majority of 55 percent.
2015 In January, 12 people are killed and 11 injured in a terrorist attack by Islamic gunmen on the Paris headquarters of *Charlie Hebdo*; in November, a series of attacks by Islamic terrorists kill 130 people and leave hundreds more wounded.
2016 Thousands take to the streets and protest against the new labour laws introduced by the government.
2017 Emmanuel Macron, leader of the radical centrist party En Marche! beats far-right Front National leader, Marine Le Pen, to win the Presidential election.
2018 France wins the FIFA World Cup.
2019 A fire destroys the roof of Notre-Dame Cathedral.
2020 A patient in a Paris hospital becomes the first person to die of Covid-19 outside Asia.
2024 Emmanuel Macron's Renaissance party defies election predictions and holds on – just – against Marine Le Pen's ascendant National Rally.

Close up of 'the Iron Lady'

Places

Paris is a compact and logically ordered city that anyone can quickly get the hang of. Its public transport networks are highly efficient, but by far the best way to get to know the city is to potter around it on foot, allowing plenty of time for aimless but often fruitful digressions. The river creates the main division, and the Right Bank (Rive Droite) and Left Bank (Rive Gauche) have their distinct, long-established associations. Right has the reputation as the powerhouse of business and commerce; Left is the historic centre of learning. There is also a traditional east-west divide between the wealthy west and poorer, more radical east. But even these boundaries are porous, and arty centres of creativity are now more likely to be in the northeast of the city than in affluent St-Germain-des-Prés, and young urban professionals are increasingly buying into the traditionally working-class parts of the city.

Administratively, the city is divided into twenty *arrondissements,* starting with the 1st in the centre (taking in Île de la Cité and the area around the Louvre) and spiralling outwards clockwise to end at the 20th in the northeast. Confusingly, while Parisians often refer to the *arrondissement* in which they live, they also refer to the historic *quartiers,* such as the Marais, Bastille or Latin Quarter, that often straddle *arrondissements* (the Marais, for example, extends into the 3rd and the 4th *arrondissements*; the Latin Quarter into the 5th and 6th).

Île de la Cité

Highlights
- **Notre-Dame**, see page 36
- **The West Front**, see page 38
- **Palais de la Cité**, see page 40
- **Palais de Justice**, see page 40
- **Other Attractions on the Île de la Cité**, see page 42

The Île de la Cité has long been the heart of Paris. During the third century BC, the Celtic Parisii tribe are thought to have set up home on this, the largest island in the Seine. In 52BC, Roman legions conquered the settlement and founded Lutetia Parisiorum on the left bank. During the Middle Ages, the island was the centre of political, religious and judicial power, not only for Paris but for the whole of France. Nowadays, it is still the geographical centre of the capital and home to several of the city's main official buildings. Sainte-Chapelle and Notre-Dame also make the island an enduring focus for religious tourism.

Notre-Dame

Dominating the island is **Notre-Dame** ❶ (www.notredamedeparis.fr; free). The site has played a religious role for at least two thousand years. In Roman times a temple to Jupiter stood here; in the fourth century AD it was replaced by a Christian church, St-Etienne; this was joined two centuries later by a second church, dedicated to the Virgin. Norman raids left them both in a sorry state, and, in the twelfth century, Bishop Maurice de Sully decided that a cathedral should be built to replace them.

The main part of Notre-Dame, begun in 1163, took 167 years to finish. Its transition from Romanesque to Gothic has been called a perfect representation of medieval architecture – an opinion that has provoked some dissent. Cistercian monks protested that such a sumptuous structure was an insult to the godly virtue of poverty, and today some architectural purists still find Notre-Dame excessive.

The original architect is unknown, but Pierre de Montreuil (who was involved in the building of Sainte-Chapelle, see page 41) was responsible for much of the thirteenth-century work. The present look of the cathedral is due to Eugène Viollet-le-Duc, who from 1845 to 1863 restored it to repair the ravages of the eighteenth century, caused more by pre-Revolutionary meddlers than by revolutionaries stripping it of religious symbols. Popular

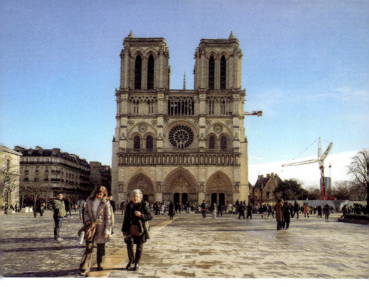

Notre-Dame

support for the expensive restoration was inspired by Victor Hugo's novel, *Notre-Dame de Paris*.

The cathedral has witnessed numerous momentous occasions over the centuries, including, in 1239, the procession of Louis IX, during which the pious king walked barefoot, carrying his holy treasure – believed to be Christ's crown of thorns. In 1594 Henri IV made his politically motivated conversion to Catholicism here to reinforce his hold on the French throne. Napoleon crowned himself emperor at Notre-Dame, upstaging the Pope, who had come to Paris expecting to do it; the scene is depicted in Jacques-Louis David's vast painting, *The Consecration of Napoleon,* now in the Louvre. Other occasions include General de Gaulle marking the 1944 Liberation of Paris with a Mass here, and in 1970 his death was also commemorated here. In 2019, a devastating fire destroyed the cathedral's roof, causing extended closure; it reopened in December 2024 after renovations.

The West Front

Across the three doorways of the west front, the 28 statues of the **Galerie des Rois** represent the kings of Judah. These are nineteenth-century restorations: the originals were torn down during the Revolution because they were thought to depict kings of France. Twenty-one of them were discovered in 1977 and moved to the Musée du Moyen Age (see page 78).

The central **rose window** depicts the Redemption after the Fall. Two more outsized rose windows illuminate the transept; the northern one retains most of its thirteenth-century glass. A fourteenth-century *Virgin and Child* is to the right of the choir entrance.

WHERE TO SHOOT THE BEST PICTURES

The Latin Quarter Riverbank - Wonderful views across the river to Notre-Dame can be enjoyed from Square Viviani. For the best photos, aim for sunrise over Notre-Dame or sunset over the Louvre.

Pont des Arts - The Pont des Arts, covered in symbolic padlocks, enjoys a reputation as 'the bridge of romance'. Take your shots from either the south or middle of the bridge, and shoot at midday, when the shadows are shortest.

Sacré-Coeur - Square Willette is a great place to take photos of the iconic Sacré-Coeur, while panoramic city views can be had from the top of the dome. Try to beat the crowds by arriving in the early morning.

The Panthéon - This former church and mausoleum is a Neoclassical masterpiece, and its interior is covered with gorgeous nineteenth-century murals. For the best exterior shots, arrive at sunrise.

Monsieur Bleu - Enjoy the height of Parisian dining culture by snapping a photo and dining at this chic restaurant inside the Palais de Tokyo gallery. The best vantage point to snap photos is from the dining room terrace.

View of the Conciergerie

The 255-step climb up the **north tower** (charge) is rewarded with glorious views of Paris and close-ups of the roof and Notre-Dame's famous gargoyles. Cross over to the south tower to see the seventeenth-century thirteen-ton tenor bell, Emmanuel, which was joined by a new tenor bell, Marie, in 2013; eight new bells were installed in the north tower at the same time. There are spectacular views from here too. Napoleon III's town planner Baron Haussmann greatly enlarged the *parvis*, or cathedral forecourt, increasing the impact of the towering west front. Excavations beneath the square have revealed walls and foundations from the Gallic, Roman and medieval eras, which now form part of an exhibition on early Paris. A copper marker set into the ground, known as the *kilomètre zéro*, is the point from which all distances from Paris to the rest of France are measured.

Palais de la Cité

The other architectural and historical highlight on the Île de la Cité is the **Palais de la Cité**, the complex of buildings that includes the Conciergerie, Sainte-Chapelle and the Palais de Justice, the headquarters of the French supreme court.

Palais de Justice

The imposing neoclassical **Palais de Justice** (www.ca-paris.justice. fr; free), heart of the French legal system, stands on the site of the Roman palace where Emperor Julian was crowned in AD 360. The lobby (Salle des Pas Perdus) is well worth a visit to catch a glimpse of the lawyers, plaintiffs, witnesses, court reporters and hangers-on.

The Conciergerie

Adjacent is the **Conciergerie** ❷ (www.paris-conciergerie.fr), which became a state prison in 1370. The 'medieval' facade is misleading; it dates from the 1850s. The building's greatest notoriety dates from the late eighteenth century: in 1793, at the height of the Terror, the Conciergerie became the antechamber of the guillotine, with around 2,500 prisoners spending their last night here (see page 25). It is now a museum to its bloody past, displaying items including a guillotine blade, the crucifix before which Marie-Antoinette prayed while captive here, and the lock used on Robespierre's cell. Look out on the Cour des Femmes, where husbands, wives and lovers were allowed a final tryst before the tumbrels came to carry off the prisoners.

> **NOTES**
>
> Behind Notre-Dame is the Mémorial des Martyrs de la Déportation (www.chemins dememoire.gouv.fr; free), a poignant memorial dedicated to the two hundred thousand French deported to concentration camps during World War II.

Exquisite stained-glass in Sainte-Chapelle

Sainte-Chapelle

Concealed in the courtyard between the Palais de Justice and the Conciergerie is the magnificent Gothic **Sainte-Chapelle** ❸ (www.sainte-chapelle.fr; charge). The chapel was constructed in 1248 to designs by Pierre de Montreuil to house holy relics, fragments of which were believed to be Christ's Crown of Thorns, bought by the pious King Louis IX (later St-Louis). The lower chapel, with its star-patterned ceiling, was used by palace servants. More impressive is the upper level, where light blazes through 15m (45ft) high glass windows separated by buttresses so slim that there seems to be no wall at all. Of the 1,134 individual pieces of glass, 720 are thirteenth-century originals.

Between 1789 and 1815 Sainte-Chapelle served various roles: as a flour warehouse in the Revolution, as a club for high-ranking dandies, then as an archive for Napoleon's Consulate. This latter role fortunately saved the chapel from projected destruction, since the bureaucrats could not think of another site in which to keep their mountains of paper.

Other Attractions on the Île de la Cité

Towards the western end of the island is the pretty, tree-shaded **square du Vert-Galant** and, beyond it, a statue of Henri IV and the restored **Pont-Neuf**, which, despite its name – 'New Bridge' – is the oldest bridge in Paris. The bridge owes its survival to its solid stone – rather than wood – construction, and it was the first bridge in Paris to be constructed without houses on it. In 1985, the Pont-Neuf hit the headlines when Bulgarian-born American artist Christo wrapped the entire structure in fabric.

At the eastern end of the island is the colourful **Marché aux Fleurs** on place Louis Lépine, opposite the Préfecture de Police and Hôtel Dieu. The latter, now a hospital, was built on the site of a medieval hospital; it was the scene of intense battles when the police rose up against the occupying Germans in 1944. In contrast to these forbidding structures, the market is an array of small glasshouses selling flowers and plants. On Sunday, the stalls become a market for caged birds.

Île St-Louis

The pedestrianised Pont St-Louis crosses from the Île de la Cité to the **Île St-Louis ❹**, an island renowned for its elegant, exclusive and astronomically expensive mansions. From the western end of the shady quai d'Orléans (at the western end of the island) there is a wonderful view of the apse of Notre-Dame. However, some pilgrims to this spot are more intent on a visit to another Parisian institution: ice-cream parlour **Berthillon** (www.berthillon.fr), at 29–31 rue St-Louis-en-l'Ile, the street that cuts through the island. It is a pretty road, dotted with boutiques and restaurants. Towards the eastern end is the baroque church of **St-Louis-en-l'Île** (www.saintlouisenlile.catholique.fr; free), notable for its fine collection of Dutch, Flemish and Italian sixteenth- and seventeenth-century art.

On the northeastern end of the island, at 17 quai d'Anjou, is the grand **Hôtel Lauzun**. Built in 1640 by Louis Le Vau, architect to Louis XIV, it is now owned by the City of Paris. It was here that the poets Théophile Gautier and Charles Baudelaire lived in 1845, and where Baudelaire wrote part of *Les Fleurs du Mal*. It currently houses the Paris Institute of Advanced Studies (www.paris-iea.fr). In the **Hôtel Lambert**, on the corner of rue St-Louis-en-l'Île, Voltaire enjoyed a tempestuous love affair with the lady of the house, the Marquise du Châtelet.

Elegant and exclusive Île St-Louis

> **MAKING THE MOST OF THE MUSEUMS**
>
> Entry charges for museums range from around €10–15, with reduced rates for children, students and pensioners. Some museums charge less on Sundays, and entrance is always free on the first Sunday of the month for the following: the Louvre, Musée d'Orsay, Centre Pompidou, Musée de l'Orangerie, Musée Rodin, Musée Picasso and Musée du Moyen Age. **The Paris Museum Pass** (www.parismuseumpass.com) gives entry to over fifty museums and monuments in Paris and its surroundings, including the Louvre and Versailles. You can buy passes valid for two, four or six consecutive days at museums, tourist offices and Métro stations.

On the island's south bank is the small **Musée Adam Mickiewicz** (by reservation only, tel: 01 55 42 83 85). A Polish poet, Mickiewicz (1798–1855) lived in Paris from 1832 to 1840 and devoted himself to helping oppressed Poles. The seventeenth-century building in which the museum is housed also includes the Polish Library and displays memorabilia of the Polish composer Frédéric Chopin.

The Louvre, Tuileries & Concorde

Highlights
- **Palais du Louvre**, see page 44
- **Musée du Louvre**, see page 45
- **Palais-Royal**, see page 48
- **The Tuileries**, see page 49
- **Place de la Concorde**, see page 51

Palais du Louvre
The Louvre was eight centuries in the making, but has retained great architectural harmony nonetheless. It was originally built as a fortress by Philippe Auguste in 1190. When Louis XIV moved his

court to Versailles, he abandoned the Louvre to artists and other squatters. The Revolutionaries made it a public museum in 1793. As the home of the *Mona Lisa,* the Louvre drew almost unmanageable crowds, until President Mitterrand ordered its reorganisation in the 1980s. A vast reception area and main entrance was excavated in the forecourt and topped by the iconic glass **Pyramid** designed by Sino-American architect I.M. Pei.

Musée du Louvre

The **Musée du Louvre** 5 (www.louvre.fr; charge; free first Sunday of the month) is divided into three wings: Richelieu in the north, Sully in the east and Denon in the south. The collections are arranged in colour-coded sections. A free map is available at the ticket desks, where an audio guide with interactive map can also be rented and the useful official mobile app can be downloaded free.

The following is a summary of the Louvre's many treasures, including some of the highlights in the different sections.

The Louvre is a masterpiece of symmetry

Lower-Ground and Ground Floors

A good place to start is the exhibition on the medieval Louvre, on the lower-ground floor of the Sully

Wing. This is where you can see the remains of Philippe-Auguste's fort and keep, and some of the artefacts discovered in the 1980s excavations. On the lower ground floor of the Denon Wing is the Department of Islamic Art, which is recognisable by its iridescent, undulating roof. Above, on the ground floor of the Sully Wing, are Egyptian and Greek Antiquities, and on the ground floor of the Denon wing are Etruscan and Roman antiquities.

The lower ground floor of the Richelieu wing showcases French sculpture, including Guillaume Coustou's giant *Horses of Marly*. The French sculpture collection continues on the ground floor of the Richelieu wing, with works spanning the fifth to eighteenth centuries. Also here are Mesopotamian finds, such as the black basalt

Inside the Louvre

Babylonian *Code of Hammurabi* (1792–1750BC), one of the world's first legal documents.

First and Second Floors

The first floor houses some of the biggest crowd-pullers. The first floor of the Denon Wing is a spectacular collection of large-format French painting, notably Delacroix's *Liberty Leading the People*, Géricault's *Raft of the Medusa* and David's *Consecration of Napoleon*. Adjacent is a room showcasing Leonardo da Vinci's enigmatic Florentine noblewoman, the *Mona Lisa* (known in French as *La Joconde*). This iconic piece, painted in 1503, is now displayed behind bulletproof glass in a special, frequently crowded room that it shares with Veronese's vast *Wedding at Cana* canvas.

At the staircase dividing the Denon and Sully wings is the *Winged Victory of Samothrace* (second century BC), a Hellenistic figurehead commemorating a victory at sea, and the glittering Galerie d'Apollon (Apollo's Gallery), home to the crown jewels. At this point you reach the Sully Wing and the graceful Hellenic statue of the *Venus de Milo* (second century BC), bought by the French government for 6,000 francs in 1820 from the island of Milos. Most of the first floor of the Richelieu Wing houses works of the decorative arts.

The whole second floor is dedicated to painting, with highlights including Dürer's *Self-Portrait*, Vermeer's *The Lacemaker,* Watteau's *Pierrot* and Ingres's *The Turkish Bath*. The Richelieu Wing houses works from Flanders, the Netherlands, Germany and France (fourteenth to seventeenth centuries); the second floor of the Sully Wing is devoted to French paintings of the seventeenth, eighteenth and nineteenth centuries.

Additional Museums

The Rohan and Marsan wings at 107–111 rue de Rivoli house the **Musée des Arts Décoratifs**, which boasts over 150,000 objects dedicated to the art of French craftsmanship and design, from the

Middle Ages to the present day, and the **Library du MAD**, which houses an extraordinary collection of books on the decorative arts, graphic arts, architecture, design, costume and fashion, the history of art and the art of gardening (www.madparis.fr; charge).

Palais–Royal

The **Palais-Royal** ❻ is directly north of the Louvre, across rue de Rivoli. Built in 1639 as Cardinal Richelieu's residence, it gained its regal title when Anne of Austria moved in with young Louis XIV. This serene, arcaded palace has a colourful past. In the days of Philippe d'Orléans, Prince Regent while Louis XV was a child, it was the scene of notorious orgies. A later duke (another Philippe) built apartments above the arcades, along with two theatres (one now the Comédie Française, see page 99), shops, gambling houses and fashionable cafés.

Despite efforts to curry favour with the revolutionaries, such as calling himself Philippe Égalité (equality), the duke ended up on the guillotine with the rest of the family. After the Revolution, the palace became a gambling den again and narrowly escaped destruction during the 1871 uprising. However, following the restoration of the monarchy (1872–76), it regained respectability. The palace now houses the Ministry of Culture, the Council of State, the Constitutional Council, some shops and the historic Le Grand Véfour restaurant (see page 120).

> **NOTES**
>
> In 1986, artist Daniel Buren installed rows of black-and-white-striped stone columns in the Palais-Royal's main quadrangle, the Cour d'Honneur.

East of the Palais-Royal is the **Banque de France**, and immediately north is the **Bibliothèque Nationale Richelieu** (www.bnf.fr; free but charge for exhibitions). The latter became a royal library in 1368, when Charles V placed 973 manuscripts in the Louvre. Most of the millions of books, engravings and ancient manuscripts it has accumulated over the centuries have been transferred to the newer national library on the Left Bank (see page 81). The old building with its splendid reading room (1863) has been transformed into a specialist research library.

The Tuileries

West of the Louvre is one of the city centre's main green spaces, the **Jardin des Tuileries** ❼ (free), commissioned in 1564 by Catherine

Arcades of the Palais-Royal

de Medici to be the garden for her new Palais des Tuileries. Tuileries were workshops that made roof tiles in the area, before the crown purchased the site and André Le Nôtre landscaped the area. The Palais des Tuileries was the formal home of the French monarchy until its destruction in the upheaval of the Paris Commune in 1871. The current gardens extend across the palace's former site.

Walk around the chestnut and lime trees, and admire sculptor Aristide Maillol's sensual statues of nymphs and languorous maidens, a few of which are coquettishly concealed behind a miniature maze. A project is currently underway to restore the gardens to their original glory and to make them even more welcoming to the 14 million people who visit them each year.

At the eastern entrance to the Tuileries is the pink **Arc de Triomphe du Carrousel**, built by Napoleon at roughly the same

Claude Monet's Water Lilies

time as the Arc de Triomphe. The latter is visible from here in a straight line beyond the Obelisk on place de la Concorde. The same axis continues into the distant haze to the skyscrapers of La Défense.

Jeu de Paume and Musée de l'Orangerie

A few surviving fragments of the Palais des Tuileries can be seen by the **Jeu de Paume**, in the northwest corner of the gardens. Once home to real-tennis courts (hence the name) and later to the collection of Impressionist paintings now displayed at the Musée d'Orsay, the building is currently the attractive showcase for the **Centre National de la Photographie** (www.jeudepaume.org; charge). The centre showcases changing exhibitions on all photographic disciplines, including major fashion retrospectives and contemporary video installations.

In the southwest corner of the Tuileries is the **Musée de l'Orangerie** (www.musee-orangerie.fr; charge). The building was originally constructed by Napoleon III to shelter the orange trees of the Jardin des Tuileries, but since the 1920s has been the showcase for eight of Claude Monet's water-lily paintings, the Nymphéas series. In these works, the Impressionist painter captured the play of colour on the pond in his Japanese garden at Giverny (see page 97) at different times of day. Monet and the Louvre's architect drafted the original plans and elevations for their display at the museum. The two vast oval rooms upstairs still show off the famous paintings to his specification. In the gallery space downstairs is the Jean Walter and Paul Guillaume Collection, an exceptional array of works by artists including Cézanne, Renoir, Matisse, Picasso, Soutine, Modigliani, Utrillo and Henri Rousseau.

Place de la Concorde

In 1753, Ange-Jacques Gabriel designed the vast **place de la Concorde** ❽ as place Louis XV, but the Revolutionaries later dispensed with all royal connotations. The King's statue was replaced with a guillotine, used to behead Louis XVI. In 1934, the square was the scene of bloody antigovernment rioting by French fascists.

In the centre of the square is a pink-granite, 23m (75ft) tall Obelisk, a gift from Mohammed Ali, viceroy of Egypt. Dating from 1300 BC and once part of the temple of Ramses II in Luxor, it was erected here in 1836.

The two horses guarding the entrance to the Champs-Élysées are replicas of the eighteenth-century *Horses of Marly,* by Guillaume Coustou (originals are in the Louvre).

NOTES

According to official estimates, 1,119 people were decapitated on place de la Concorde, including Louis XVI, his queen Marie-Antoinette, Charlotte Corday, the poet André Chénier and, ironically, even the Revolutionary leader Robespierre.

Overlooking the Grands Boulevards

The Grands Boulevards

Highlights
- **Palais Garnier**, see page 53
- **Madeleine**, see page 53
- **Place Vendôme**, see page 55

North of the Louvre and Tuileries are the Grand Boulevards, a line of wide avenues running from west to east. The boulevards date from the seventeenth century, when Louis XIV tore down the medieval walls around Paris and created broad, tree-lined spaces. In the nineteenth century Baron Haussmann extended the string westwards, and the western end of what was named boulevard Haussmann became the preserve of the rich. High-street clothing chains now dominate stretches of the central boulevards, although traces of Second Empire extravagance can still be seen in the ornate balconies and facades.

Palais Garnier

Dominating the place de l'Opéra is the city's historic opera house, the **Palais Garnier** ❾ (www.operadeparis.fr), where opera and ballet are performed in tandem with the newer Opéra Bastille (see page 62).

In 1860 architect Charles Garnier was commissioned by Napoleon III to build an opera house. His lavish designs were truly in tune with the pomp and opulence that characterised the Second Empire. A six-ton chandelier dominates the five-tiered auditorium, which is dripping with velvet and gilt. Marc Chagall painted the auditorium ceiling in 1964. Tours also take in the library and museum, showcasing scores, costumes and sets.

Madeleine

A stock exchange, the Bank of France, a theatre; these were among the uses proposed for the huge neoclassical church of **La Madeleine** ❿ (www.eglise-lamadeleine.com; free), on place de la Madeleine. Building first began in the eighteenth century,

The Vendôme column

The inside-out Centre Pompidou

but stalled until Napoleon commissioned the current church in the nineteenth century as a temple to the glory of his army. Its colonnaded exterior with a heavily sculpted pediment, emulates a Roman temple such as the Maison Carrée in Nîmes. La Madeleine's political role was eventually muted when the Arc de Triomphe was built. The restored monarchy opted to use the Madeleine as a church, and the building was finally consecrated in 1842. Climb the steps for great views down rue Royale to place de la Concorde and the Assemblée Nationale.

Place de la Madeleine is home to luxury food shops, including Fauchon (nicknamed 'millionaire's supermarket') and truffle retailers Maison de la Truffe. Also on the square is the **Kiosque-Théâtre Madeleine** (www.kiosqueculture.com), where you can buy half-price seats for same-day theatre shows.

Place Vendôme

Louis XIV wanted this square to be an imposing setting for a monument to him, but after it was laid out in 1699, only his financiers could afford the rent. Today the Ministry of Justice shares the square with banks, jewellers and the Ritz hotel. The statue of Louis XIV was overthrown during the Revolution. Its replacement, the Vendôme column, commemorates the victories of Napoleon and is modelled on Trajan's Column in Rome. Cast from 1,250 Austrian cannons captured at Austerlitz, it is topped by a statue of the emperor. Like him, it was toppled, in the 1871 Commune (see page 27) at the instigation of the painter Gustave Courbet, who had to pay to have it re-erected two years later.

Beaubourg, Les Halles & the Marais

Highlights
- **Châtelet and Hôtel de Ville**, see page 55
- **Centre Pompidou**, see page 56
- **Les Halles**, see page 58
- **The Marais**, see page 58

Sandwiched between the Louvre and Palais-Royal to the west and the Marais to the east, Beaubourg and Les Halles form one of the city's busiest commercial and cultural centres. The biggest landmark is the Centre Pompidou, Paris' modern art museum. For centuries, the Marais district was home to Paris's aristocrats. Today, it is an elegant, characterful district, with fine mansions, museums, attractive boutiques, kosher grocers, gay bars and hip cafés bundled together in a labyrinth of narrow streets.

Châtelet and Hôtel de Ville

Busy Place du Châtelet is a good starting point for exploring the area. Flanked by two theatres (Théâtre de la Ville and Théâtre du

Châtelet), the square lies above one of Paris' biggest Métro and RER stations.

Opening out at the eastern end of avenue Victoria is the wide esplanade of the **Hôtel de Ville** ⓫ (www.paris.fr; free), the ornate home of the city council. The neo-Renaissance building, with its magnificent Mansard roof, was rebuilt after the seventeenth-century town hall was destroyed by fire in the 1871 Commune. In medieval times, place de l'Hôtel de Ville was the site of hangings and executions, but today, the pedestrianised square is considerably more alluring, especially in the evening when the fountains are floodlit. A temporary ice-skating rink is set up here every winter for picture-perfect twirls on the ice.

Centre Pompidou

'That'll get them screaming,' said then-President Georges Pompidou, as he approved the plans for the cultural centre bearing his name. The **Centre Pompidou** ⓬ (www.centrepompidou.fr; charge) was built by architects Richard Rogers, Renzo Piano and Gianfranco Franchini, and its inside-out design, dominated by external pipes, tubes, scaffolds and escalators, caused controversy when unveiled in 1977. The pipes are not just for show: the blue ones convey air, the green ones carry water, the yellow ones contain the electrics, and the red ones conduct heating.

The building, more popularly known as Beaubourg after its thirteenth-century neighbourhood, houses a cinema, library, design centre, music 'laboratory' and museum. Such a unique building poses unique maintenance challenges, however, and from late 2025 until 2030, the Centre Pompidou is closing for renovations, with all its galleries relocated (from 2026) to a new building in the suburb of Massy (6 Av. du Maréchal Koenig).

The plaza outside is a popular rendezvous point and the site of the Stravinsky Fountain, featuring colourful sculptures by Niki de Saint Phalle.

One of the world's finest collections of twentieth-century art, the **Musée National d'Art Moderne** (National Museum of Modern Art; charge) is housed on the fourth and fifth floors, with the fifth floor home to modern works from 1905 to the 1960s, and the fourth floor covering contemporary work from the 1960s to the present day. Highlights of the modern period include works by Kandinsky, Klee, Klein, Matisse, Picasso and Pollock, and sections on Dadaism, Bauhaus and Surrealism. The contemporary collection includes pieces by Andy Warhol, Verner Panton, Joseph Beuys, Gerhard Richter and Jean Dubuffet. On level six are temporary exhibitions and the fashionable, minimalist – and expensive – *Georges* restaurant (www.beaumarly.com).

The revamped Forum des Halles

Included in the price of the ticket to the Musée National d'Art Moderne is a visit to a reconstruction of sculptor Constantin Brancusi's studio, **Atelier Brancusi**.

Les Halles

For centuries this was the site of the capital's main food market, but to widespread regret, the nineteenth-century iron-and-glass pavilions were demolished in 1971. The market is now located out of town, near Orly. The much disliked partly subterranean **Forum des Halles** shopping centre took its place, along with its gardens and playgrounds. These were swept away as part of a colossal renovation programme that was completed in 2018. A huge 2.5 hectare (6.2 acre) undulating glass and metal roof (the Canopée) now covers the Chatelet Les Halles métro hub and the Forum shopping mall, which is the largest in Paris, with 127 stores and 22 restaurants. A cultural centre as much as a shopping destination, the complex also includes a library, hip hop centre, rehearsal rooms, an academy of music and a cinema. Near Les Halles is the Renaissance **Fontaine des Innocents**, once part of a cemetery. Bars and restaurants line the adjoining rue Berger and the streets leading off it. Some of the side streets have a seedy feel, and nearby rue St-Denis, once primarily a red-light district, still has a number of sex shops.

The church of **St-Eustache** (www.saint-eustache.org; free) dominates the north side of Les Halles. Built from 1532 to 1637, the main structure is late Gothic with an imposing Renaissance colonnade on its western facade. The church stages free organ recitals at 5.30pm on Sundays.

The Marais

This district, to the north of the Île de la Cité and Île St-Louis, has successfully withstood the onslaught of modern construction. It provides a remarkably intact record of the development of the city, from the reign of Henri IV at the end of the sixteenth century to the advent of the Revolution. Built on reclaimed marshland, as its name suggests (*marais* means 'swamp'), the **Marais** contains some of Europe's most elegant Renaissance mansions (*hôtels*), many of which now serve as museums and libraries. In the 1960s, the government designated the area an historical monument, and conservation and restoration took hold. The big change in the last thirty years has been the steady influx of trendy boutiques and gay bars.

Take the métro to Rambuteau and start at the corner of rue des Archives and rue des Francs-Bourgeois, named after the poor (not bourgeois at all) who were allowed to live here tax-free in the fourteenth century. The national archives of the Ancien Régime are stored in an eighteenth-century mansion, the **Hôtel de Soubise** (www.archives-nationales.culture.gouv.fr; free). Across a vast, horseshoe-shaped courtyard, you come across the rococo style of Louis XV's time in the apartments of the Prince and Princess of Soubise.

The place to go for falafel in the Jewish quarter of Le Marais

A short walk north of here, with its entrance on rue Réaumur, is the wonderful **Musée des Arts et Métiers** ❸ (www.arts-et-metiers.net; charge) – nothing, in fact, to do with 'arts and trades', but instead Europe's oldest science museum. It has a vast collection of treasures ranging from ancient clocks and barometers to the first ever steam-powered vehicle, an enormous 1938 TV set and dozens of vintage cars, all housed in a former Benedictine priory.

A Cluster of Museums

The Marais is home to a number of prestigious museums, including, on rue des Francs-Bourgeois, the grand **Musée Carnavalet** ⓮ (www.carnavalet.paris.fr; charge), which charts the history of the city. The museum is housed in the magnificent Hôtel Carnavalet, which was once home to the lady of letters Madame de Sévigné.

Musée Carnavalet

Nearby at 5 rue Thorigny, the truly excellent **Musée National Picasso** ⓯ (www.museepicassoparis.fr; charge) is set within the restored Hôtel Salé. The museum's collections include more than two hundred paintings, 158 sculptures and hundreds of drawings, engravings, ceramics and models for stage sets and costumes drawn from the artist's personal collection, as well as works by Braque, Matisse, Miró, Degas, Renoir and Rousseau.

Another Marais museum, housed in the Hôtel Donon at 8 rue Elzévir, is the **Musée Cognacq-Jay** (www.cognacq-jay.paris.fr; charge), which contains a splendid collection of eighteenth-century paintings, furniture and *objets d'art*, bequeathed to the city by the founders of La Samaritaine. This grand old department store (at Châtelet), known for its impressive Art Deco interior, was closed in 2005, ostensibly for safety reasons. The current owner, luxury goods conglomerate LVMH, is converting it into a department store, luxury hotel, Cheval Blanc, as well as 96 social housing units, offices and a crèche.

There are a number of other hôtels of note in the district that are closed to the public (although sometimes open on Heritage Days), but can still be admired from the outside. These include the Hôtel d'Albret, Hôtel d'Aumont and Hôtel de Beauvais. The Hôtel de Sens, the oldest mansion in the Marais, now houses the Bibliothèque Forney and occasionally has exhibitions on the decorative arts that are open to the public, as is the garden. The **Hôtel de Sully** (www.hotel-de-sully.fr; charge) houses the Centre des Monuments Nationaux but the peaceful garden is open to the public. There is also a library and bookshop.

Place des Vosges

Rue des Francs-Bourgeois ends at what many agree is the most attractive residential square in Paris, **place des Vosges** (originally place Royale). Henri IV had it laid out in 1605 on the site of an old horse-market, the idea being to have 'all the houses in the same symmetry'. After the wedding festivities of his son Louis XIII, the gardens became the fashionable place in which to promenade, and later, a spot for aristocratic duels.

The Romantic writer Victor Hugo lived at No. 6, now a **museum** (www.maisonsvictorhugo.paris.fr; charge) housing a small collection of his artefacts. It is worth visiting to see the interior of one of the square's grand mansions.

> **NOTES**
>
> Since its launch in 2007, the city council's Vélib' automated cycle hire scheme has steadily grown and improved. There are over 1,800 stations across the capital and 30 percent are electric. The bikes are utilitarian but in good working order and prices are reasonable. For details, visit www.velib-metropole.fr.

Jewish Quarter

As the Marais has become popular with bar and boutique owners, the Jewish community has retreated to a small pocket centred on Rue des Rosiers, which is lined with kosher delis and falafel stands. Jewish history is told at the **Musée d'Art et d'Histoire du Judaïsme** ❿ (www.mahj.org; charge) on rue du Temple. The **synagogue**, with its Art Nouveau facade by Hector Guimard, is at 4 rue Pavée.

Bastille & Eastern Paris

> **Highlights**
> - **Bastille**, see page 62
> - **Eastern Paris**, see page 63

For years a run-down area, Bastille was given a shot in the arm by the construction of a new opera house in the late twentieth century. The area south of here, Bercy, has since become a potent symbol of urban regeneration, with a disused nineteenth-century railway viaduct and dilapidated wine warehouse district brought back to life and now thriving.

Bastille

No trace of the prison stormed in 1789 remains on the **place de la Bastille**. Even the column in the centre commemorates a later revolution, that of 1830. The area was largely ignored, until the **Opéra Bastille** ⓱ (www.operadeparis.fr), one of Mitterrand's *grands projets* (see page 29) was built. Cutting-edge artists and designers, like Jean-Paul Gaultier, moved into the area, and now, in streets such as rue de la Couronne, traditional shops alternate with galleries and cool restaurants. North of the Bastille are rue Oberkampf and rue Jean-Pierre Timbaud, where there is a concentration of hip bars and boutiques.

To the south of the Bastille are the quirky shops and cafés of Canal St-Martin, while at 1–129 avenue Daumesnil is the **Viaduc des Arts**

Enchanting Place des Vosges

(www.leviaducdesarts.com). In the golden age of rail, the Viaduc de Paris, built in 1859, supported a train line from Bastille to the Bois de Vincennes. However, as the railways declined in the twentieth century, the viaduct fell into disrepair. It was saved from demolition and reopened in 1998, with attractive glass-fronted workshops, fashion and craft boutiques occupying its arches.

Eastern Paris

In **Bercy**, old stone-walled warehouses and cobbled streets have been given a new lease of life in the shape of Bercy Village, centred on cour St-Emilion, home to boutiques, restaurants and cafés. On the north side of the Parc de Bercy, a repurposed Frank Gehry building became the new home of the **Cinémathèque Française**, housing a film museum, research centre, repertory cinema, restaurant and film archive. Pedestrians and cyclists can cross to the Left Bank on the Passerelle Simone de Beauvoir.

Also northeast of the Bastille is the colourful neighbourhood of **Belleville**, home to an attractive park with panoramic views of Paris and one of the city's two Chinatowns.

Champs–Élysées, Trocadéro & West

Highlights
- **Champs-Élysées**, see page 65
- **Arc de Triomphe**, see page 66
- **Trocadéro**, see page 67
- **Western Paris**, see page 69
- **Bois de Boulogne**, see page 70
- **Around Monceau**, see page 70

The **Champs-Élysées** ⑱ were designed by landscape architect André Le Nôtre in 1667 as an extension of the Tuileries (see page 49). Initially the promenade only reached as far as the Rond-Point des Champs-Élysées, less than half its current length. Over

PÈRE LACHAISE CEMETERY

The Cimetière du Père Lachaise (www.paris.fr/dossiers/bienvenue-au-cimetiere-du-pere-lachaise-47 free) has seen an estimated 1,350,000 burials since its foundation in 1804. It even served as a battleground in 1871, when the Communards made a last stand here: the Mur des Fédérés in the southeast corner marks the place where many of them were executed by firing squad. Tombs of the famous include those of the painter Ingres, dancer Isadora Duncan, composers Rossini and Chopin, and writers such as Molière, Balzac, Proust and Oscar Wilde; the latter honoured with a fine monument by Jacob Epstein. Other famous names include singers Edith Piaf and Jim Morrison, and actress Marie Trintignant.

a hundred years passed before the rest of the avenue, stretching up to the Arc de Triomphe, was completed. Its reputation has ebbed and flowed with the centuries, and it is currently experiencing something of a comeback as one of the city's most prestigious shopping strips.

Champs–Élysées

The commercial stretch of the **Champs-Élysées** runs from the Rond-Point to the Arc de Triomphe. The landmark stores are a four-storey, multi-brand shopping arcade, LE66, at No. 66;

The Champs-Élysées seen from the top of the Arc de Triomphe

Guerlain at No. 68, with its Rococo-style facade and sumptuous interior; Sephora - an Aladdin's cave of beauty products - at No. 70–72; Louis Vuitton at No. 101.and at No. 53, the Atelier Renault, which has a swish mezzanine restaurant and cocktail bar.

The majority of designer shops are concentrated around avenue Montaigne, the southern end of avenue George V and rue du Faubourg St-Honoré. This is high fashion land, where prices are sky-high.

On the southern side of the Champs, between place Clémenceau and the river, is the imposing, glass-domed **Grand Palais** ❶ (www.grandpalais.fr; open during exhibitions only; charge), constructed for the 1900 World Fair. The Grand Palais hosts several major art exhibitions every year; the colossal building also houses the

> **NOTES**
>
> Renowned in Paris for generations for its delectable macaroons, Ladurée (www.laduree.fr), a bakery/restaurant at 75 avenue des Champs-Élysées, is always busy and very chic. Don't leave without trying the melt-in-the-mouth macaroons, which come in a multitude of flavours. There are other branches in the city.

Palais de la Découverte (www.palais-decouverte.fr; charge), which includes a hands-on exhibition of the sciences, with a planetarium as centrepiece.

Across avenue Winston Churchill is the **Petit Palais**, which houses the fine-art collection of the Musée des Beaux-Arts de la Ville de Paris (www.petitpalais.paris.fr; charge).

Arc de Triomphe

The circular area at the top of the Champs-Élysées is popularly known to Parisians as *l'Etoile* (the star), after the twelve avenues branching out from its centre. Officially renamed **place Charles de Gaulle** after the death of the president in 1970, it is dominated by one of the most familiar Paris icons, the **Arc de Triomphe** [20] (www.monuments-nationaux.fr; charge). The arch is 50m (164ft) high and 45m (148ft) wide. A trip to the top of the staircase (lift for the disabled only) affords excellent views. It is from here that you can best appreciate the *tour de force* of geometric planning that the avenues represent.

Napoleon I conceived of the Arc de Triomphe as a tribute to his armies, and it bears the names of hundreds of his marshals and generals, and dozens of victories. No defeats are recorded, naturally, although a few of the victories are debatable. Napoleon himself only ever saw a wood-and-canvas model, since the arch was not completed until the 1830s. It rapidly became the focus for state occasions, such as the return of the emperor's remains from St Helena in 1840 and the funeral of Victor Hugo in 1885. At the Liberation, this was the spot where General de Gaulle began his triumphal march down the Champs-Élysées.

Under the arch is the grave of the Unknown Soldier. Since 1920, it has been the last resting place of a soldier who died in World War I. The eternal flame was lit here in 1923.

Trocadéro

Dominating place du Trocadéro is the **Palais de Chaillot** ㉑, built for the Paris World Fair of 1937. The imposing Art Deco palace was designed in the shape of an amphitheatre, with its wings following the original outline of the old Trocadéro in graceful symmetry. The west wing is home to the **Musée National de la Marine** (www.musee-marine.fr; charge). Also here is the Musée de l'Homme (www.museedelhomme.fr; charge). The east wing houses the **Cité de l'Architecture et du Patrimoine** (www.citedelarchitecture.fr; charge), which combines Paris's old architecture museum with the Institut Français d'Architecture.

On avenue des Nations-Unies is the **Aquarium de Paris** (www.aquariumdeparis.com; charge), a vast aquarium with cinema and animation studio. There are dozens of tanks containing some nine thousand fish, grouped in mini marine ecosystems.

Arc de Triomphe

Down avenue du Président Wilson is the vast **Palais de Tokyo** ㉒, built as the Electricity Pavilion for the 1937 World Fair. One wing was intended to hold post-1905 fine art from the municipal fine-art collection; the other wing (now the Site de Création Contemporaine) was planned for the national collection of modern art. The **Musée d'Art Moderne de la Ville de Paris** (www.mam.paris.fr; free, charge for exhibitions) opened there in 1961. In 1977 the core collection of French and international art was given a new home at the Centre Pompidou. Whereas the emphasis at the Centre Pompidou is on international art, here the focus is on artists who worked in Paris.

In the other wing is the **Site de Création Contemporaine** (www.palaisdetokyo.com; charge), where a multi-disciplinary

The Musée d'Art Moderne de la Ville de Paris

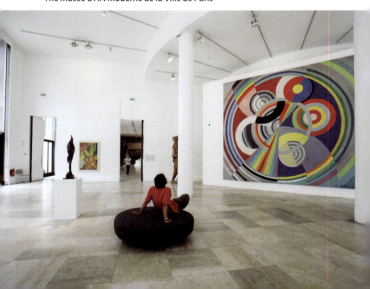

> **APP HAPPY**
>
> With the ubiquity of smartphones, it is no surprise that Paris has some very handy apps for use on the go. One of the best is the RATP public transport authority's slick, free guide to its entire network, with live traffic updates, maps and route planning capabilities. Heetch works in the same way as Uber, but solely for late-night travellers, from 8pm to 6am. Le Fooding Guide is created by Parisians and has recommendations for the best places to eat in the city. Another free guide is produced by the Louvre, and has maps of the museum and useful background on its most popular exhibits. Secrets de Paris reveals a different gem every day – from hidden streets to obscure monuments.

programme focuses on young artists through exhibitions, performances and workshops.

Opposite the Palais de Tokyo to the north is the Palais Musée de la Mode-Galliera de la Ville de Paris (10 avenue Pierre 1er de Serbie; www.palaisgalliera.paris.fr; charge), which houses the city's collection of clothes and accessories dating from the eighteenth century to the present day.

Western Paris

West of the Palais de Chaillot, Passy is an upmarket, villagey residential area with a couple of busy shopping streets (rue de Passy and rue de l'Assomption). It is also home to the atmospheric **Maison de Balzac** (www.maisondebalzac.paris.fr; 47 rue Raynouard; charge). Balzac penned much of his great opus *La Comédie Humaine* here.

Also in the west of Paris is the **Musée Marmottan-Monet** (www.marmottan.fr/en, 2 rue Louis-Boilly, charge), showcase for the art assembled by collector Louis Marmottan (1856–1932). The displays are comprised mostly of Impressionist masterpieces, including works by Monet, Renoir, Manet and Gauguin, but there is also some exceptional First Empire furniture.

Bois de Boulogne

In western Paris is the capital's biggest park, comprising 900 hectares (2,200 acres) of grassland, lakes and woods. Inspired by Hyde Park in London, Napoleon III commissioned Baron Haussmann to transform a remnant of an old hunting forest into a public park. The plans included the **Bagatelle**, once a royal retreat, which now has both manicured and English-landscape style gardens. Also within the park is a craft museum, a boating lake, the **Jardin d'Acclimatation** (www.jardindacclimatation.fr; charge) amusement park with attractions for children, and two racecourses: Longchamp for flat races; Auteuil for steeplechases. However, parts of the park after dark are considered to be among the most dangerous places in Paris. Adjacent to the park is the $143 million futuristic building of **Fondation Louis Vuitton** (www.fondationlouisvuitton.fr), opened in 2014. Designed by the famous architect Frank Gehry, it gives shelter to a museum, exhibition spaces, bookstore and restaurant.

Sacré-Cœur

Around Monceau

Overlooking Parc Monceau, the **Musée Nissim de Camondo** (63 rue de Monceau; http://madparis.fr/Musee-Nissim-de-Camondo-742; charge) was built by a wealthy Jewish banking family in the style of the Petit Trianon (see page 95) at Versailles. The remarkable collection of tapestries, carpets, porcelain, furniture and paintings, all dating from the eighteenth century, were bequeathed to the state in 1935 by the passionate art collector, Count Moïse de Camondo, in memory of his son, Nissim, killed in action in 1917. The building and family history are as fascinating as the collection.

Also beside Parc Monceau is the **Musée Cernuschi** (7 avenue Vélasquez, www.cernuschi.paris.fr; free, charge for temporary exhibitions), one of the most important collections of Oriental art in Europe. The nineteenth-century financier Henri Cernuschi amassed the collection on a tour of China and Japan, and built this mansion to house it.

South of Parc Monceau, at 158 boulevard Haussmann, is the **Musée Jacquemart-André** ❷ (www.musee-jacquemart-andre.com; charge). The museum displays art and furniture that once belonged to wealthy collector Edouard André and his wife, erstwhile society portrait painter Nélie Jacquemart. The house is magnificent, and its fine-art collection includes works by Bellini, Boucher, David, Donatello, Uccello, Rembrandt and Titian. The gorgeous café, decorated with chandeliers and antiques, is also worth a visit.

Montmartre & Pigalle

Highlights
- **Sacré-Cœur**, see page 72
- **Place du Tertre**, see page 73
- **Pigalle**, see page 73

With narrow, winding streets and dead-ends, **Montmartre** ('*la Butte*', or the hill, to its residents) still has something of a provincial feel. For over two hundred years it has been associated with artists and bohemians. The tourist *Montmartrobus* (www.ratp.fr) spares you the walk and shows you some of the area in a single sweep,

The Moulin Rouge – you can't miss it

but the best way to discover Montmartre at your own pace is to start early, at the top. Take the Métro to Abbesses and the lift to the street (the stairs here seem endless) – and note the handsome Art Nouveau entrance as you leave. Rue Yvonne le Tac leads to the base station of a funicular railway.

Sacré-Cœur

The funicular (Métro/bus tickets are valid) climbs to the terrace right in front of the Byzantine-style basilica of **Sacré-Cœur** ❷❹ (www.sacre-coeur-montmartre.com; charge for crypt and dome). Standing at the highest point in Paris, it is one of the city's principal landmarks; for many, the best reason to visit the basilica is the view of the city from the dome or the terrace below. The Sacré-Cœur's white appearance comes from the local Château-Landon limestone, which bleaches on contact with carbon dioxide in the air and hardens with age.

Place du Tertre

A few steps west of Sacré-Cœur is **St-Pierre-de-Montmartre**, one of the city's oldest churches. Consecrated in 1147, it is a significant work of the early Gothic style, belied by its eighteenth-century facade. Nearby **place du Tertre** was once the centre of village life. The square is best visited early in the morning, before the pushy portrait artists set up their easels and the crowds of tourists take over.

On place Emile Goudeau, just downhill but artistically on an altogether much higher level, No. 13 was the site of the studio known as the **Bateau-Lavoir** (so-called because the building resembled the Seine's laundry boats until it was destroyed by fire). It was here that Picasso, Georges Braque and Juan Gris developed Cubism, Modigliani painted, and Apollinaire wrote his first Surrealist verses. Some of their predecessors – Renoir, Van Gogh and Gauguin – once lived and worked just north of place du Tertre.

The **Cimetière de Montmartre** ㉕ (free) is at 20 avenue Rachel. The cemetery's more illustrious tenants include composers Berlioz and Offenbach, the sculptor Degas, German poet Heinrich Heine and film director François Truffaut.

Pigalle

At the far end of rue Lepic, a market street renowned for its food shops and several appealingly bohemian cafés, is place Blanche, where the ambience changes. On the corner of boulevard de Clichy is the iconic **Moulin Rouge** (www.moulinrouge.fr; charge), that first opened its doors in 1889 and is still staging its entertaining nightly cabarets, although these days that's mostly to tourists. Next door is **La Machine du Moulin Rouge** (www.lamachinedumoulinrouge.com), a huge nightclub, pumping with the sounds of house, dance music and mainstream pop.

Less artistic attractions abound in **Pigalle**, a powerhouse of the Paris sex trade for decades. Tasselled curtains provide glimpses of smoky interiors, garish signs promote live sex shows and pushy bouncers attempt to entice passers-by.

However, Pigalle's sleaze has been tempered by trendy nightlife venues. The cabarets that formerly occupied half the houses along rue des Martyrs are increasingly being taken over by hip clubs and fashionable bars.

La Villette

In northeast Paris, right against the Périphérique ring road, is the **Parc de la Villette** ❷ (Métro: Porte de Pantin or Porte de la Villette, http://lavillette.com; charge). Laid out on the site of an enormous abattoir, which was rendered obsolete by improved refrigeration techniques and poor design (the cows could not get up the steps), 55 hectares (136 acres) of futuristic gardens surround a colossal science museum, the **Cité des Sciences et de l'Industrie** (www.cite-sciences.fr; charge).

La Géode

Begin at 'L'Univers' (Universe), which has a spectacular planetarium and also provides an explanation of the Big Bang. 'La Vie' (Life) is an eclectic mix of medicine, agriculture and economics.

> ### ALONG THE CANAL
>
> The Paris canals were dug in 1821 as a transport link for the factories and warehouses in the area northeast of the Bastille. Shielded by trees, the canal is a popular strolling ground, particularly on balmy summer evenings. A pleasant way to experience it is by canal boat, starting either at Bastille or at La Villette. Canal tours lasting around two and a half hours are run by Canauxrama (www.canauxrama.com).

'La Matière' (Matter) reproduces a nuclear explosion and gives you the chance to land an Airbus 320, and 'La Communication' has displays of artificial intelligence, three-dimensional graphics and virtual reality. On the ground floor is the Cité des Enfants, which has interactive exhibits and activities for children aged 2–12 years. Outside the main entrance is L'Argonaute, a retired naval submarine.

La Géode (www.lageode.fr; charge) is a giant silver ball housing a wraparound IMAX cinema. The former cattle market now houses a cultural and conference centre in the immense nineteenth-century Grande Halle. Next door, the **Cité de la Musique - Philharmonie de Paris** is an edifice of angles designed by architect Christian de Portzamparc, and includes the **Musée de la Musique** (http://philharmoniedeparis.fr; charge). Portzamparc also designed the national music and dance conservatory on the other side of the Grande Halle. The museum charts the development of classical, jazz and folk music and houses an impressive collection of over 4,500 musical instruments.

The impressive gardens of the park are the biggest to be built in Paris since Haussmann's time. Designed by Bernard Tschumi and opened in 1993, they comprise several thematic areas such as the Jardin des Frayeurs Enfantines (Garden of Childhood Fears) with a huge dragon slide, and the Jardin des Vents (Garden of Winds), home to multicoloured bamboo. Abstraction continues in the form of

Tschumi's folies: red angular 'tree houses' (minus the trees), each with a special function such as play area, workshop, daycare centre or café.

Latin Quarter & St-Germain-des-Prés

> **Highlights**
> - **The Latin Quarter**, see page 76
> - **St-Germain-des-Prés**, see page 81
> - **Odéon**, see page 84

The area referred to as the Latin Quarter lies to the east of boulevard St-Michel. This maze of ancient streets and squares has been the stamping ground of students for nearly eight centuries and it is home to the city's most famous university, the Sorbonne. Latin was virtually the mother tongue until Napoleon put a stop to it after the Revolution. West of boulevard St-Michel is St-Germain-des-Prés, once the centre of literary Paris and existentialism, with the oldest church in Paris at its heart. Although these two areas have changed over the past few decades, with high fashion increasingly replacing heavy thinking, they still maintain their charm in tree-lined boulevards, narrow streets and beautifully manicured gardens.

The Latin Quarter

Begin your viist to the Latin Quarter at **place St-Michel**, where students buy their books or gather around the grand 1860s fountain by Gabriel Davioud with a statue of the archangel Michael stamping on the devil. From here, plunge into the narrow streets of the **St-Séverin** quarter to the east (rues St-Séverin, rue de la Huchette, de la Harpe and Galande). Here, you will find medieval streets teeming with Greek restaurants, Tunisian bakeries selling sticky date pastries, independent art-house cinemas and student bars.

The early Gothic church of **St-Julien-le-Pauvre** (143 545 216; free), located on the street of the same name, hosts regular recitals of chamber and religious music. Just across rue St-Jacques stands the exquisite thirteenth- to fifteenth-century flamboyant Gothic church of **St-Séverin**, in which Dante is said to have prayed and French composer Camille Saint-Saëns asked to be made honorary organist. Outside, look for a hefty slab of brownish stone by the well, to the right of the entrance; it is all that remains of the paving of the Roman thoroughfare now replaced by rue Saint-Jacques.

Second-hand book stall

The Sorbonne

Named after the thirteenth-century college established by Robert de Sorbon for poor theological students, the university was later taken in hand by Cardinal Richelieu, who financed its reconstruction (1624–42). Very few of the somewhat forbidding buildings are open to the public, but you can go inside the seventeenth-century **courtyard** with its ornate sundial and see the outside of the Baroque library and domed church. It is one of the most prestigious universities in the world.

Protests against overcrowding, antiquated teaching, bureaucracy and the basis of the social system made the Sorbonne a focal point for unrest in 1968, a year of ferment across Europe. Over on the tree-shaded **place de la Sorbonne**, it is hard to imagine the police invading such a peaceful sanctuary, one that for centuries guaranteed student immunity. But invade they did, and revolt

Musée National du Moyen Age

exploded onto the streets. Students and workers made common cause, and there followed widespread national strikes that threatened the survival of the government. In the aftermath of the revolts, the Sorbonne was absorbed into the huge Paris Universities monolith and lost its independence.

Musée National du Moyen Age – Thermes de Cluny

Opposite the Sorbonne's rue des Ecoles entrance is the **Musée National du Moyen Age** ㉗ (6 place Paul-Painlevé; www.musee-moyenage.fr; charge), still often called by its former name, the Musée de Cluny. Once the residence of the Abbots of Cluny, the museum houses one of the world's finest collections of medieval artefacts. Its star attraction is the exquisite, fifteenth-century tapestry *La Dame à la Licorne* (The Lady and the Unicorn), six pieces depicting the five senses and the temptations that the eponymous lady vows to overcome. The museum also holds 21 of the original heads of the Kings of Judah, sculpted in 1220 for Notre-Dame cathedral, but vandalised during the Revolution.

The Hôtel de Cluny was built on the remains of a huge Gallo-Roman bath house believed to have been erected in AD 200 by the guild of *nautes* (boatmen); ships' prows are carved on the arch supports of the frigidarium (cold bath house).

Panthéon

Designed in 1755 as the church of Ste-Genviève (patron saint of Paris), the neoclassical **Panthéon** ❷❽ (www.paris-pantheon.fr; charge) was requisitioned during the Revolution to serve as a mausoleum. In the nineteenth century its status oscillated between secular and sacred, but Victor Hugo's funeral in 1885 settled the issue in favour of a secular mausoleum. The interior is sparse, its walls covered with nineteenth century murals by Puvis de Chavannes. The crypt is a maze of corridors lined with cells containing tombs.

Rue Mouffetard

The old streets behind the Panthéon, where the bustling **rue Mouffetard** and its offshoots meet, are like a small town within the city. The stalls of rue Mouffetard's morning market are piled with appetising produce. Here, and on tiny **place de la Contrescarpe** nearby, you will find restaurants serving a wide range of international cuisine. A little to the east, signs to **Arènes de Lutèce** point to a little park that is the site of a Roman amphitheatre, partially restored after its remains were found in the nineteenth century.

On rue St-Etienne-du-Mont is the church of **St-Etienne-du-Mont** (www.saintetiennedumont.fr; free). This was the parish church of the Abbey of Ste-Geneviève and still houses a shrine to the city's patron saint. The highlight is the Renaissance rood screen (1541), the only one in Paris.

Institut du Monde Arabe

Back by the Seine, but heading east, stroll past the university complex that stands on the site of the former Halles aux Vins (wine

> **NOTES**
>
> Among those interred in the Panthéon are novelist Emile Zola, socialist Jean Jaurès, Louis Braille and Pierre and Marie Curie.

market). Designed by architect Jean Nouvel, the nearby **Institut du Monde Arabe** ㉙ (1 rue des Fossés-St-Bernard; www.imarabe.org; charge) was built with the help of 16 Arab nations to foster cultural links between Europe and the Islamic world. Inside, a museum traces the cultures of the Arab world with first-rate exhibits. A library of over forty thousand volumes covers all aspects of Arab culture. There are two restaurants (Le Zyriab has fine views), a literary café and a bookshop.

Jardin des Plantes

Adjacent is the **Jardin des Plantes** (www.jardindesplantes.net; charge), created by Louis XIII in the early seventeenth century as 'a royal garden of medicinal plants'. Today it is a tranquil space and a fine botanical and decorative garden, with a huge variety of exotic plants flourishing in its greenhouses. The oldest tree in Paris is located here, too.

Institut du Monde Arabe

The adjoining **Muséum National d'Histoire Naturelle** (www.mnhn.fr; charge) has renovated its venerable exhibits of fossils, skeletons, butterflies and mineral samples. The **Grande Galerie de l'Evolution** (36 rue Geoffroy-St-Hilaire; charge), devoted to the origins of life on earth, is outstanding.

NEW LEFT BANK

The 'new' Rive Gauche is the biggest urban renewal project since the mid-1850s. Newly created streets and buildings are going up in a zone of rusty factories and disused railway tracks that extend south along the river from the Gare d'Austerlitz. The area's centrepiece is the **Bibliothèque Nationale de France François Mitterrand** (www.bnf.fr; charge), opened in 1996; its 90m (300ft) high glass towers evoke open books. Nearby, at 34 quai d'Austerlitz, the concrete warehouses that once belonged to Paris's central port have been rebuilt as **Les Docks – Cité de la Mode et du Design** (www.citemodedesign.fr; free), whose bright green riverfront facade is unmissable and houses a fashion school, the Institut Français de la Mode (www.ifm-paris.com), as well as multiple exhibition spaces, bars, clubs and restaurants.

St-Germain-des-Prés

Once the heart of literary Paris, **St-Germain-des-Prés** covers an area stretching roughly from St-Sulpice to the Seine and bounded to the west by boulevard St-Germain. Its elegant streets house chic boutiques, yet it still retains a sense of animation, with crowded cafés spilling out onto the pavements. In the 1950s the area became a breeding ground for literature and philosophy. Writers such as Jean-Paul Sartre, Simone de Beauvoir and Albert Camus, gathered at **Les Deux Magots**, **Café de Flore** and other venues to discuss existentialism.

That said, the days of black polo-necks and beret-clad existentialists engaged in heated debate are over. The area has been colonised by designer shops, especially in the streets around the carrefour de la Croix Rouge and place Saint-Sulpice and upmarket antiques dealers dominate the side closest to the river. The Marché St-Germain now contains boutiques, a swimming pool, an auditorium and a food market. On the opposite side of the boulevard, the church of **St-Germain-des-Prés** ❸⓿ (http://

eglise-saintgermaindespres.fr; charge) is the oldest in Paris, parts of it dating from the eleventh century.

Académie Française

The august Palais de l'Institut de France, home of the **Académie Française**, is north of the church of St-Germain, on quai de Conti by the Pont des Arts. It was designed by Louis le Vau in 1668 to harmonise with the Louvre across the river. The Institut began as a school for the sons of provincial gentry, financed by a legacy from Cardinal Mazarin. Then, in 1805, the building was turned over to the Institut, which comprises the Académie Française, supreme arbiter of the French language founded by Cardinal Richelieu in 1635, and the Académies des Belles-Lettres, Sciences, Beaux-Arts, and Sciences Morales et Politiques.

Les Deux Magots

Musée Delacroix and St–Sulpice

Tucked away in a tiny square a short walk from the church of St-Germain-des-Prés is the delightful **Musée National Eugène Delacroix** ㉛ (6 place Furstenberg; www.musee-delacroix.fr; charge). The painter lived here from 1857 to 1863 while he was working on frescoes in a chapel at St-Sulpice. Temporary exhibitions are held in the airy former studio, and letters

The Jardin du Luxembourg

and personal effects are displayed in the house. There is a wonderfully calm garden out the back.

A short hop south across boulevard St-Germain-des-Prés is place St-Sulpice, the eastern side of which is dominated by Jean-Baptiste Servandoni's Italianesque church of the same name. **St-Sulpice** (www.paroissesaintsulpice.paris; free) is notable for its vast towers, one of which is higher than the other, and for Delacroix's massive oil-and-wax frescoes, completed only two years before his death.

Jardin du Luxembourg

The beautifully landscaped **Jardin du Luxembourg** ㉜ is the quintessential Paris park. Students read, relax or play tennis, old men meet under the chestnut trees to play chess or a game of *boules*, lovers huddle together on metal chairs, and children sail boats across the carp-filled pond and ride a merry-go-round designed by Charles Garnier, architect of the historic opera house (see page 53). At the northern end of the gardens, the Italianate **Palais du Luxembourg** (guided tours one Saturday each month; www.senat.fr), built for Marie de Médicis in the early seventeenth century, now houses the French Senate. The adjacent Petit Luxembourg is the official home of the president of the Senate.The **Musée du Luxembourg** (19 rue de Vaugirard; www.museeduluxembourg.fr; charge) hosts art exhibitions.

Odéon

The Odéon district lies between the Latin Quarter and St-Germain-des-Prés. Across boulevard St-Germain, at the Carrefour de l'Odéon, a statue of the Revolutionary leader Georges Danton marks the spot where his house once stood. Fellow Revolutionary Camille Desmoulins lived at No. 2 before storming the Bastille in 1789. Others plotted to the north in neighbouring streets that now shelter some of the most expensive boutiques and apartments in Paris.

From here, rue de l'Odéon, the first street in Paris to have gutters and pavements, leads to place de l'Odéon. The neo-classical **Odéon Théâtre de l'Europe** (www.theatre-odeon.eu; show times vary), founded in 1782, is home to one of France's leading state theatre companies. It puts on a repertoire of mainly foreign playwrights (Büchner, Chekhov, Shakespeare, etc), sometimes in original-language productions.

Around the Eiffel Tower

Highlights
- **Musée d'Orsay**, see page 85
- **Assemblée Nationale**, see page 86
- **Musée Rodin**, see page 87
- **Les Invalides**, see page 87

Orsay's vast central sculpture aisle

- **The Eiffel Tower**, see page 88
- **Musée du Quai Branly**, see page 90

When the Paris nobility moved out of the Marais in the eighteenth century, and Versailles dwindled, the rich and famous built new town houses across the river from the Tuileries, in the 7th *arrondissement*. Not only is this chic district rich with upmarket architecture, it also has a wealth of visitor attractions, with highlights including the Musée d'Orsay, the Eiffel Tower, the Invalides and the Musée Rodin.

Musée d'Orsay

'The station is superb and truly looks like a Fine Arts Museum, and since the Fine Arts Museum resembles a station, I suggest… we make the change while we still can,' said painter Edouard Detaille in 1900. In 1986, his joke became a reality. Linked to the Tuileries by the Passerelle Léopold-Sédar-Senghor footbridge, the converted nineteenth century hotel-cum-railway station was transformed into the **Musée d'Orsay** ❸ (www.musee-orsay.fr; charge), devoted to French art from 1848 to 1914. Keeping the exterior much as it was, Italian architect Gae Aulenti adapted the interior to house many of the previously scattered works of that period, including the superb Impressionist collection formerly held in the Jeu de Paume (see page 50). Sculpture is well represented, and photography is covered from its inception (1839) onwards.

Many visitors start at the top with the Impressionists who include Renoir, Cézanne, Manet and Monet, before heading down to the mezzanine for the Post Impressionists, notably Van Gogh and Gauguin. Among the ground-floor collections, the vast canvases of Gustave Courbet are outstanding. Rest weary feet at Café Campana, high up behind the huge old station clock, or the beautifully restored Restaurant du Musée d'Orsay on the second floor.

Napoleon's tomb inside the Église du Dôme

Assemblée Nationale

Geographically if not temperamentally part of the Left Bank, the **Palais Bourbon** is the seat of the **Assemblée Nationale** (126 rue de l'Université) the Lower House of the French Parliament. Built from 1722 to 1728 for Louis XIV's daughter the Duchess of Bourbon, it forms a fittingly stately riverside facade for the grand 7th *arrondissement*. Built in the style of the Grand Trianon at Versailles, Napoleon later added the Grecian columns facing the Pont de la Concorde. The palace is more graceful when seen from its entrance on the south side. Only French citizens can go in, apart from on the annual Journées du Patrimoine open days, when thousands queue to see the Delacroix paintings in the library.

Musée Rodin

The Prime Minister's residence, Hôtel Matignon (57 rue de Varenne), is a short walk from the Assemblée Nationale. Its private park has a music pavilion favoured for secret strategy sessions. On the same elegant street, at No. 77, Rodin's former mansion, the delightful 18th-century Hôtel Biron, is now a showcase for the sculptor's works in the form of the **Musée Rodin** ❹ (www.musee-rodin.fr; charge). Many of the most famous sculptures are in the gardens (Oct–Mar closure at 5pm). Highlights include *The Kiss* (removed from the Chicago World Fair of 1893 for being too shocking), *The Thinker* (reputedly Dante contemplating the Inferno), *The Burghers of Calais and Balzac,* depicting the writer as a mountain of a man. Also on display are works by Camille Claudel, the most famous of Rodin's mistresses.

Les Invalides

One of the most important sights in this area is the monumental **Hôtel des Invalides** ❺ (www.musee-armee.fr; charge), established by Louis XIV as the first national hospital and retirement home for soldiers wounded in action. At one time it housed some six thousand veterans, but Napoleon Bonaparte commandeered a large part of the building for the superb **Musée de l'Armée** (www.musee-armee.fr), a vast collection of weapons and military paraphernalia dating from medieval times to the modern era. It is, in effect, several museums in one: there are large sections devoted to the two world wars, as well as intricate eighteenth century models of French towns and fortresses, suits of armour, and uniforms.

Les Invalides came to symbolise the glory of Napoleon himself, when his remains were brought back from St Helena in 1840 for burial in the chapel under the golden **Eglise du Dôme**. The emperor's son, who died of tuberculosis in Vienna, is buried in the crypt; his remains were sent here by Hitler in 1940.

The main courtyard allows access to the adjoining church of **St-Louis-des-Invalides**, decorated with flags taken by French armies in battle. The courtyard itself contains the 18 cannons, including eight taken from Vienna, which Napoleon ordered to be fired on great occasions, including the birth of his son in 1811. The cannons sounded again for the 1918 Armistice and the funeral of Marshal Foch in 1929.

Southwest of the Invalides is the **Ecole Militaire**, where officers have trained since the middle of the eighteenth century. Their former parade ground, the vast **Champ de Mars**, a green space stretching all the way to the Eiffel Tower.

The Eiffel Tower

For many, the ultimate Paris monument is still the **Tour Eiffel** ❸❻, or Eiffel Tower (www.toureiffel.paris; charge). When Gustave Eiffel's icon was chosen as the centrepiece of the World Fair of 1889, he claimed enthusiastically, 'France will be the only country with a 300m flagpole!' But his designs were met with strong opposition. The architect of the opera house, Charles Garnier, and the novelist Guy de Maupassant were its most vocal opponents; Maupassant organised a protest picnic underneath it – 'the only place out of sight of the wretched construction'.

However, the Paris public loved their new tower, and only a few years later writers and artists such as Apollinaire, Jean Cocteau, Raoul Dufy and Maurice Utrillo heaped praise upon it. At 321m

(1,054ft) the tower was the world's tallest building until 1931, when New York's Empire State Building went up. Surviving a proposal for its demolition in 1909, when the placing of a radio transmitter at the top gave it a valuable practical function, the tower is climbed by some 7 million visitors a year.

There are 360 steps to the first floor, where there are audio-visual presentations on the tower's history, a vertigo-inducing glass floor 57m (187ft) from the ground and restaurants, shops and the CinEiffel 'immersion show' in the Ferrié Pavilion. There are another seven hundred steps to the second floor (both first and second floors accessible by lifts, although queues are likely), which has the two-Michelin-starred Jules Verne restaurant, shops and even a

The iconic Eiffel Tower

A colourful mural in Montparnasse

macaroon bar. At the very top of the tower, (accessible by lift only) is a glassed-in viewing platform and open-air section, a champagne bar and Gustave Eiffel's office. On a clear day panoramas of over 65km (40 miles) can be enjoyed (see page 127). On hot days the ironwork expands, enabling the tower to grow as much as 15cm (6in). Even in the strongest of winds, it has never swayed more than 12cm (4in). Up to 40 tonnes of paint have to be used when it is painted every seven years.

Musée du Quai Branly

Just northeast of the tower, at 37 quai Branly, is Jacques Chirac's cultural legacy, the **Musée du Quai Branly** ❼ (www.quaibranly.fr; charge). The museum houses a collection of around 300,000 objects of art from Africa, Asia, the Americas and Oceania, with over 3,600 items actually on display. With its colonial overtones, the collection has sparked some controversy, but the building itself – a striking foliage-covered scarlet edifice designed by Jean Nouvel – has been more warmly received.

Montparnasse

Named after the mountain home of the classical Muses, 'Mount Parnassus' was a mound left after quarrying. In the 1920s, the quarter took over from Montmartre as the stamping ground of the city's artistic colony, led by Picasso. American expatriates such as Ernest Hemingway, Gertrude Stein, F. Scott Fitzgerald and John Dos Passos liked the free-living atmosphere and added to the mystique themselves.

One of Henry Miller's hangouts, Le Select (99 boulevard du Montparnasse) opened as an all-night bar in 1925. *Les Six*, the group of composers that included Milhaud, Poulenc and Honegger, met here. La Coupole (see page 127), just opposite, at No. 102, was a favourite with literary couple Sartre and de Beauvoir in the years following World War II. Le Dôme at No. 108 has lost some of its character since the days of Modigliani and Stravinsky, with elaborate remodelling. Across the street, at No. 105, La Rotonde was where Picasso, Derain and Vlaminck used to meet. At the junction of boulevard du Montparnasse and boulevard St-Michel, La Closerie des Lilas is where Lenin and

> **NOTES**
>
> Beneath Montparnasse are the city's catacombs (1, avenue du Colonel Henri Rol-Tanguy - entrance on place Denfert-Rochereau; www.catacombes.paris.fr; charge), old quarries whose corridors were used for the reburial of millions of skeletons from overcrowded cemeteries and charnel houses. Unidentified, the bones are stacked on shelves or artfully arranged into macabre patterns.

Trotsky dreamt of a Russian Revolution, and where Hemingway and his friends met after World War I.

Today the attraction isn't immediately evident: boulevard du Montparnasse is plain by Paris standards, and most of the haunts where the 'Lost Generation' found itself have been polished and painted, or even entirely rebuilt. But people still pay elevated prices for the privilege of sitting in a seat that may have been warmed by Modigliani, Lenin or Sartre.

The 59-storey, 210m (689ft) **Tour Montparnasse** (33 avenue du Maine; www.tourmontparnasse56.com; charge) may be something of an egregious eyesore, but the view from the top is marvellous. Gourmets should visit Le Ciel de Paris, which claims to be the highest panoramic restaurant in Paris.

The **Cimetière du Montparnasse** ❸❽ (entrance on boulevard Edgar Quinet; free) contains the tombs of composers Saint-Saëns and César Franck, writer Maupassant and poet Baudelaire, plus Alfred Dreyfus, the Jewish army officer whose conviction on trumped-up spying charges split the nation. Also buried here are car-maker André Citroën, Vichy Prime Minister Pierre Laval (executed while dying from a suicide attempt), philosopher Jean-Paul Sartre and writer Simone de Beauvoir.

La Défense

Follow the long avenue de la Grande-Armée down from the Arc de Triomphe, and the battery of towers looms larger and larger beyond the elegant, leafy suburb of Neuilly. Cross the river and you are in a mini-Manhattan that has grown since 1969 to become a mini-city in its own right.

The **Grande Arche** ❸❾ is further away than most of the towers, and only when you get close do you realise how big it is. A hollow cube 110m (360ft) high and 106m (347ft) wide, it could straddle the Champs-Élysées and tuck Notre-Dame underneath it. Built with remarkable speed (Danish architect Johann-Otto von Sprekelsen

Lunch on the steps under the Grande Arche

won the contest in 1983 and the arch was completed in time for the bicentennial of the French Revolution in 1989), the Grande Arche stands in line with the Arc de Triomphe and the Louvre. Its white gables are clad in Carrara marble, the outer facades in a combination of grey marble and glass. The two 'legs' contain offices, and the roof houses conference rooms and exhibition spaces. Increasing numbers of visitors and office workers have given rise to a growing number of shops, cinemas, hotels and restaurants at La Défense. Most are concentrated in the **Quatre Temps** shopping centre (www.les4temps.com), which also includes the 16-screen UGC Ciné Cité La Défense cinema complex (www.ugc.fr).

Across the main concourse, a 12m (39ft) bronze thumb by César literally sticks out like a sore thumb. Stroll down the tiers of terraces and you will discover even more statues, fountains and murals by

Miró, Calder and other modern artists, all detailed on street-plans from the Espace Défense (15 place de la Défense; www.ladefense.fr). Here you can also find out about the history of the area and the plans for Norman Foster's Hermitage Plaza, due to complete in 2027.

Excursions

Highlights
- **Versailles**, see page 94
- **Fontainebleau**, see page 95
- **Malmaison**, see page 96
- **Vaux-le-Vicomte**, see page 96
- **Giverny**, see page 97
- **Disneyland Pari**, see page 97

Versailles

Louis XIV's palace at **Versailles** ❹ is as extravagant as the Sun King was himself. A visit to the château takes most or all of a day and entails a lot of walking. Versailles is 24km (15 miles) southwest of Paris, by road (N10), by train from Gare St-Lazare to Versailles-Rive Droite, or by RER (line C) to Versailles-Rive Gauche. Various ticket combinations are available on the website: www.chateauversailles.fr.

Highlights of the interior include: the baroque **Royal Chapel**; the **State Apartments**, in which Louis XIV entertained; the Salon de Diane, where he played billiards; the 73m (240ft) long **Galerie des Glaces** (Hall of Mirrors); and the King's Bedroom, where Louis died of gangrene in 1715. In the Queen's Bedroom, nineteen royal children were born, the births often attended by members of the court, as was the custom.

The grandest facade faces west to the gardens, where the fountains spout to music at weekends (Apr–Oct). The **Grand Trianon**, the small palace Louis XIV used when he wanted to escape the vast

The Galerie des Glaces at Versailles

château; the **Petit Trianon**, favoured by Louis XV and the **Hameau** and miniature farm are also worth a visit. The Hameau was built as a place of lesiure in a vernacular, rustic style for Marie-Antoinette.

Fontainebleau

The seat of sovereigns from Louis IX to Napoleon III and a glittering example of French Mannerism, the château at **Fontainebleau** ㊶ (www.chateaudefontainebleau.fr; charge) makes a pleasant day trip. Here Louis XIV signed the Revocation of the Edict of Nantes in 1685, and Napoleon I signed his first act of abdication in 1814. gloriously chaotic profusion of styles – a showcase of French architecture from the twelfth to the nineteenth centuries. At the very heart of the palace, the secretive and splendidly asymmetrical Cour Ovale conceals a twelfth-century fortress keep, jarringly but pleasingly flanked by fine Renaissance wings on either side. Take time to wander through the gardens – including André Le Nôtre's Grand Parterre, the largest formal garden in Europe. Fontainebleau is 64km (40 miles) southeast of Paris by the A6 or by train from Gare de Lyon, then Ligne A bus to the château.

Malmaison

Set in lovely grounds, the château at **Malmaison** ㊷ (http://musees-nationaux-malmaison.fr/chateau-malmaison; charge) was the home of Napoleon's wife, Josephine, who continued to live here after their divorce. Many of her possessions are on display. Malmaison is 6km (4 miles) west of Paris. Métro: Grande Arche de La Défense, then bus 258, or RER to Rueil-Malmaison, followed by bus Optile 27.

The original Japanese bridge in Monet's garden

Vaux-le-Vicomte

This seventeenth-century château (www.vaux-le-vicomte.com; charge) was designed by Louis Le Vau, André Le Nôtre and Charles Le Brun for Louis XIV's finance minister, Fouquet. No sooner was it completed than the king had its owner arrested for embezzlement and jailed for life. **Vaux-le-Vicomte** ㊸ (http://vaux-le-vicomte.com; charge) is 55km (35 miles) southeast of Paris on the N5 or by train from Gare de Lyon to Melun, then a taxi ride.

Giverny

Claude Monet lived at this house in **Giverny** ㊹ (www.fondation-monet.com; charge) from 1883 to 1926 and painted the gardens many times, especially the water lilies (see the Musée de l'Orangerie, page 51). Giverny is situated 85km (53 miles) northwest of Paris by the A13, D181 and D5, or by train from Gare St-Lazare to Vernon, with a shuttle bus from the station to Giverny.

> **NOTES**
>
> Cityrama ParisVision (www.pariscityvision.com) runs day trips from Paris to Fontainebleau and Vaux-le-Vicomte as well as guided tours and candlelit visits.

Disneyland Paris

Disneyland Paris ㊺ (www.disneylandparis.com; charge) encompasses a theme park, hotels, restaurants, a convention centre, a golf course, tennis courts and swimming pools; and attracts over 16 million visitors a year. In the theme park itself, Main Street USA recaptures the traditions of small-town America at the turn of the twentieth century, and leads to four other 'lands' – Frontierland, Adventureland, Fantasyland and Discoveryland. Each themed section has a variety of fun experiences to offer. Every evening there is a parade including floats inspired by the famous Disney movies. In the **Walt Disney Studios Park** visitors can explore film sets; the Twilight Zone Tower of Terror thrill ride ends with a sheer drop into a black hole. It is worth using the Premier Access scheme (charge; available online) to beat the queues.

The resort is 32km (20 miles) east of Paris, near Marne-la-Vallée. A motorway gives access from the city and the airports, Charles-de-Gaulle and Orly. Speedy commuter trains (RER line A) from the capital and even faster long-distance trains (TGV) serve Marne-la-Vallée/Chessy station near the entrance.

The charming Passage Jouffroy in the 9th district dates from 1836

Things to Do

Critics of Paris sometimes dismiss it as a 'museum city', a conglomeration too reverently preserved in aspic. Nothing could be further from the truth. The past matters, but this is also one of the liveliest and most influential cultural powerhouses in the world, with an enormous army of contemporary creators and outlets for film, theatre, music and fashion. It's also a consumer paradise, with some of the best shops you'll find anywhere.

Culture

Art

Paris is one of the world's great art cities. The **Musée de Louvre** alone (www.louvre.fr/en; charge) stakes a claim to being the planet's most famous art gallery, and is home to inarguably the world's best-known painting, the *Mona Lisa*. There is somewhere in the region of 130 art galleries to choose from across the city, but given limited time, stick to a few which you can devote a decent amount of time and attention to.

The Louvre aside, some of the city's best art institutions include the **Musée National d'Art Moderne** (www.mam.paris.fr/en; charge), housed within the Centre Pompidou, and the **Musée National Picasso** (www.museepicassoparis.fr/en; charge), home to the world's largest collection of works by Pablo Picasso.

Theatre

The main national theatre is the **Comédie Française** (1 place Colette; www.comedie-francaise.fr), where works by revered seventeenth-century French writers such as Molière (comedy) and Racine (tragedy) are performed. Modern classics are also shown here and at the **Théâtre du Vieux Colombier** (21 rue du Vieux-Colombier; tel: 144 581 515); the **Théâtre du Châtelet** (2 rue

Edouard Colonne, www.chatelet-theatre.com) hosts opera, classical concerts and the occasional ballet.

Opera and Ballet
Opera and ballet are staged in the lavish **Palais Garnier** (place de l'Opéra) and in the modern **Opéra Bastille** (place de la Bastille). www.operadeparis.fr.

Jazz, Pop and Rock
Paris has excellent jazz credentials and a long list of clubs. An established venue is the **Caveau de la Huchette** (5 rue de la Huchette; www.caveaudelahuchette.fr). **Le Sunset/Sunside** (60 rue des Lombards; www.sunset-sunside.com) is two jazz clubs in one: electric jazz and world music, plus acoustic. Bigger names perform at **New Morning** (7 & 9 rue des Petites-Ecuries; www.newmorning.com) and the **Jazz Club Etoile** (Le Méridien; 81 boulevard Gouvion-St-Cyr; www.jazzclub-paris.com).

Pop and rock concerts are held at the **Zénith** in the Parc de la Villette (see page 74), the **Stade de France**, Parc des Princes, and the **AccorHotels Arena** (see page 107). Ticket offices (*billeteries*) at branches of the Fnac chain (www.fnac.com) will have details of who is playing.

Nightlife
For event listings, check *L'Officiel des Spectacles* (www.offi.fr). The Wednesday supplement of *Le Figaro* is another good source. Up-to-date information can also be found at http://parisjetaime.com/eng.

Clubs and Bars
The words 'Paris nightlife' make many visitors think of Montmartre and Montparnasse, but these days the biggest after-dark buzz is around rue Oberkampf in the east of the city. **Café Charbon** (109

rue Oberkampf; www.lecafecharbon.fr) launched the area's nightlife boom two decades ago and is still going strong; behind it is the same management's **Nouveau Casino** one of the liveliest nightclubs in the city. Nearby **L'Alimentation Générale** (64 rue Jean-Pierre Timbaud; www.alimentation-generale.net) is a cavernous bar with club nights and world music concerts.

Exciting venues are not confined to the east. **Showcase** (Pont Alexandre III) is a club underneath the Right Bank end of the Pont Alexandre III, which attracts a trendy young crowd.

In the centre of town, film director David Lynch set up the city's first members' bar, the very swanky and atmospheric **Club Silencio** (142 rue Montmartre; www.silencio-club.com); non-members can get in after 11pm. Another big-name central drinking den is **Harry's Bar** (5 rue Daunou). Hemingway, Gershwin and others frequented this authentic Paris institution. The cocktails are excellent – and strong.

Further north, and with a more youthful, electro vibe, is **Point Ephémère** (200 quai de Valmy; www.pointephemere.org), set on the bank of the Canal St-Martin a short walk southwest from Jaurès Métro station. This clubbing and concert venue also has a good restaurant and café, a waterfront terrace in summer, and a gallery.

Point Ephémère

La Samaritaine department store

The Marais is arguably the hippest neighbourhood in Paris, where fashion, art and the gay scene mix, with institutions like Raidd (23 rue du Temple) and hip hideaways such as **Little Red Door** (60 rue Charlot; www.lrdparis.com).

For information about clubs and concerts, pick up the free, fortnightly pocket magazine *Lylo* (www.lylo.fr) in trendy bars and music shops.

Cabarets

Lavish nearly-nude cabarets, geared mainly for tourists, hark back to the capital's 'naughty' image of yesteryear. The **Lido** (116 bis av. des Champs-Élysées; www.lido.fr) and the **Folies Bergère** (32 rue Richer; www.foliesbergere.com) are classic survivors. **Crazy Horse** (12 av. George V; www.lecrazyhorseparis.com) puts on slick yet knowingly tongue-in-cheek shows. The celebrated **Moulin Rouge** (82 blvd de Clichy; www.moulinrouge.fr) puts on two shows a night.

Shopping

The range of shops in Paris is vast. There are the eye-poppingly expensive jewellers on elegant place Vendôme, the high fashion icons in St-Germain-des-Prés, the much-loved book stalls on the banks of the Seine, and the ever-popular flea markets on the edges of the city. There's also an enduring tradition of small, specialist retailers.

> **NOTES**
>
> Paris is a famously foodie city, and every *quartier* has its *chocolatiers*, superb *pâtisseries* and *boulangeries* (bakers), *boucheries* (butchers), delicatessens, ripe-smelling *fromageries* (cheese shops) and bustling street markets.

What to Buy Where

Each neighbourhood has its own mood and atmosphere, and the shops often reflect its history and the people who live there. In terms of fashion, expect boho designers in Montmartre; designer couture on **rue du Faubourg-St-Honoré** and **avenue Montaigne**; and cool, contemporary streetwear around rue Etienne-Marcel. The exclusive 7th *arrondissement* is good for traditional menswear, along with upmarket interior design boutiques. Chic place Vendôme glitters with diamond-encrusted baubles, but you will find more original pieces in St-Germain-des-Prés or the Marais. Opulent antiques are sold around quai Voltaire in the 7th and rue du Faubourg-St-Honoré in the 8th. Retro furnishing and ceramics from the 1960s and '70s are popular near Bastille and Montmartre.

That said, the shopping map of Paris is far from static, reflecting an ebb and flow that goes with the rise and fall of different areas. The Champs-Élysées, which zigzagged from the epitome of glamour in the early twentieth century to that of tourist dross in the 1980s, started returning to favour in the 1990s, and is now buzzing with upmarket brands including multi-brand store LE66 (www.le66.fr). Historically staid rue St-Honoré is now the focus for a more avant-garde fashion set and, similarly, designer fashion has migrated to once-literary St-Germain-des-Prés.

Since the 1990s, restoration of its beautiful *hôtels particuliers* and the installation of several important museums have transformed the **Marais** into a highly international district with youthful fashion boutiques and cutting-edge design shops. Rue Charlot, in the 3rd, is a hive of contemporary fashion activity, while the hub of the Marais' fashionable area around rue Vieille-du-Temple has a wealth of independent bookshops and clothing stores.

The bookshop in la Halle Saint Pierre in the 18th

Some neighbourhoods reflect the changing population of Paris. In the 13th *arrondissement*, with its large South-East Asian population, you'll find Chinese supermarkets and *pâtisseries* among the high-rise tower blocks. Another overlooked corner over in the 10th, the **Canal St-Martin** has resolutely made its mark on the retail map, highlighted by the three colourful shops of quirky fashion retailer Antoine et Lili.

Other areas have not fared as well: the aristocratic history of the boulevards of Bonne Nouvelle and Montmartre is now a distant memory smudged by discount stores and fast-food chains. **Forum des Halles**, right in the heart of the city, used to be the epitome of retail decline, with its three-level underground shopping mall long reviled for its array of brash chain stores, but after a huge regeneration project, the ugly 1970s Forum building has been replaced by a gleaming new cultural and shopping complex, together with a pretty park, which is partially sheltered by a massive green glass canopy. It currently boasts 127 stores, including exclusive brands such as L'Exception and Celio, together with 22 restaurants, a cinema, a gym, an Olympic-sized swimming pool, a media library and a hip-hop centre.

Markets

The city's markets pull in bargain hunters, foodies and collectors alike. There are three main flea markets: in the 18th *arrondissement*, the famous **Marché aux Puces de St-Ouen**, which is the largest of its kind in the world, the smaller **Marché aux Puces de la Porte de Vanves**, and, in the 12th *arrondissement*, the **Marché d'Aligre**. Slightly down-scale, but every bit as popular, is the **Puces de Montreuil** market in the 20th *arrondissement*. Roving street markets (Marché Volant) are held in various locations across the city a few mornings a week (usually from about 7am up until the early afternoon); at these you can find authentic produce and a distinctive local character.

Open-air swimming session by the banks of the Seine

In addition, there are over fifty street markets; some have just a few stalls, whereas others, such as Marché Bastille or Marché de l'avenue Daumesnil, stretch for hundreds of metres and have a superb range of stock. Market streets, including rue Mouffetard, in the Latin Quarter, have food shops with stalls that spill onto the pavement and are open all day from Tuesday to Saturday, with a long break for lunch, and on Sunday morning. For more information, see https://parisjetaime.com.

Sports

The city caters fairly well for the sports enthusiast. You can find details on sporting events in the Wednesday edition of *Le Figaro*. For comprehensive information about sporting facilities visit http://parisjetaime.com.

Spectator Sports

Football and rugby fans can watch games at the huge **Stade de France** (rue Francis de Pressensé, St-Denis; www.stadefrance.com) just north of the city ringroad. The **Parc des Princes** (22 rue du Commandant Guilbaud; www.psg.fr) is home to Paris's premier division football team, Paris St-Germain. The huge **Accor Arena** (8 boulevard de Bercy; www.accorarena.com/en), and now hosts events such as ice skating, motor sports, basketball, handball and tennis. It can hold up to 20,300 spectators.

For horse racing, the Grand Prix de l'Arc de Triomphe takes place in October, at **Longchamp** in the Bois de Boulogne.

Participant Sports

The few public tennis courts in Paris, such as those at the Jardin du Luxembourg, are available on a first-come-first-served basis. Municipal swimming pools include the **Piscine Josephine Baker**, which floats on the Seine and has a retractable roof for warm weather. For details of municipal sports facilities, see http://parisjetaime.com. The quais de Seine, Bois de Boulogne and Canal St-Martin offer good cycling opportunities; the **Fédération Française de Cyclotourisme**, http://ffvelo.fr, has details of cycling clubs.

Children

For most children, Disneyland (www.disneylandparis.com; see page 97) will be far more appealing than any city sightseeing. For a cheaper alternative, an afternoon in one of Paris's parks (see pages 49 and 83) might do the trick. For small

> **NOTES**
>
> Major sporting events include the Six Nations Cup in Feb/March, the Marathon in April, and the French Tennis Open in May/June at the Stade Roland-Garros.

Bastille Day celebrations

children there are merry-go-rounds, puppet theatres (not Jul–Aug), pony rides and toy boats in the **Jardin du Luxembourg**. The **Jardin d'Acclimatation** (see page 70) is a children's park with a zoo, pony rides and puppet shows in the Bois de Boulogne. For the scientifically minded, there is a lot to learn in the **Cité des Sciences et de l'Industrie** (see page 74), where the Cité des Enfants is aimed at children aged 2–12. Kids can also get hands on with science at the **Palais de la Découverte** (see page 66) on the Champs-Élysées.

Festivals and events

For more details of the below and other events, see http://paris jetaime.com
January Chinese New Year celebrations, Chinatown. Métro: Porte d'Ivry.

Spring Foire du Trône (late March–early May), a monster funfair at Pelouse de Reuilly, Bois de Vincennes, Métro: Porte Dorée.
April Paris Marathon ends on the Champs-Élysées.
Good Friday The Archbishop of Paris leads Procession of the Cross up the steps of Sacré-Cœur basilica, Montmartre, Métro: Anvers.
May/June French Open Tennis Championships, chic Grand Slam event, Roland-Garros stadium, Métro: Porte d'Auteuil.
June For the Fête de la Musique (Music Festival) on the 21st, there are free concerts all over Paris.
July Bastille Day (14th). Festivities include a military parade along the Champs-Élysées, a firework display at the Trocadéro and dancing on place de la Bastille. The Tour de France ends on the Champs-Élysées. Paris Cinéma, international film festival, screenings at various venues. Night-time firework displays and illuminated fountains at the Château de Versailles (mid-July–mid-Sept).
July/August Paris-Plages, the wildly successful 'city beach' brings sand, palm trees and a host of open-air attractions and entertainment to the banks of river and canal for four weeks. See www.paris.fr.
September Journées du Patrimoine, open days at otherwise off-limits government and private buildings.
October Prix de l'Arc de Triomphe, France's biggest horse race, Longchamp, Bois de Boulogne, Métro: Porte d'Auteuil and free shuttle-bus. Festival d'Automne, the annual festival of theatre, music and dance (until December). Nuit Blanche, museums and cultural venues open late on the first Saturday of the month, with special events laid on. See www.paris.fr.
November The arrival of Beaujolais Nouveau (third Tuesday of the month) is celebrated in bars and restaurants.
December Christmas markets, La Défense and Champs-Élysées. Notre-Dame is packed for 11pm Christmas Eve Mass. New Year's Eve crowds pour onto the Champs-Élysées, and there are fireworks at the Trocadéro.

Food and Drink

Paris is considered one of the culinary capitals of the world, and deservedly so. In the early twenty-first century, the French capital's dining scene was criticised for being slow to evolve, unlike other competitors on the international stage. Such concerns have been more or less neutralised by the steady rise of regional and international cuisines, the runaway success of a number of young owner-chefs, and by the global slow food movement. Even plant-based restaurants now have a strong foothold here, in what was long a scene dominated by carnivores. Street food, by contrast, has never taken off in Paris in the same way as it has in other major

A Paris favourite

European cities; in a culture where the dining table has an almost sacred status, eating on the go is still frowned upon.

The downside is that eating out in Paris is more expensive than ever, and good bargain bistro fare – the sort of thing visitors to Paris used to rave about on their return home – is harder to find. Consult the list of recommendations in this guide (see page 120) and get the lowdown on the latest new openings in the free weekly guide *A Nous Paris* (www.anousparis.fr), available on Mondays in Métro stations. Websites Le Fooding (www.lefooding.com) and Paris By Mouth (www.parisbymouth.com) and app The Fork are all worth checking out for local recommendations.

Top 10 Things to Try

1. Bistro Dining
The bistro is the archetypal place for everyday dining in France, and Paris has the best concentration in the country. Classic options include steak frites, oysters, foie gras, boeuf bourguignon, steak tartare, coq-au-vin and sole meunière. And then comes dessert: *tarte tatin, mousse au chocolat, îles flottantes, and so much more*.

2. Parisian Breakfast
The typical 'Parisian' breakfast (*petit déjeuner*) is still croissant, brioche or bread and butter with coffee, tea or hot chocolate. Increasingly, orange juice is offered as an extra, but you must insist on orange *pressée* if you want it freshly squeezed.

3. Cheese
The concept of *terroir* (the quality and individual characteristic of the land) prevails in French cheese, as it does in wine. The regional repertoire is formidable, from creamy Camembert to cheeses rind-washed in beer or the blue-veined champions Roquefort and Bleu d'Auvergne. Each region in France has its own speciality but you'll

A profusion of French cheese

find all of them, and more, at the *fromageries* (cheese shops) all over Paris.

4. Sweet Treats
Often, the chic decor of the Parisian pâtisserie (almost) matches the decadent flavours of its offerings. These include, among other things, mousses and custards, Chantilly cream, bite-sized cakes, tarts, ice cream, cream cheese, profiteroles, *crème brûlée*, sweet crêpes, and parfaits.

5. Marché Volant Fare
The French take pride in the local produce on sale at their markets. The fishmonger does not just sell fish – he or she may offer a recipe for, say, grilling sardines in vine leaves. The fruit and vegetable

merchant knows which potato variety is best suited to a gratin, and if you ask whether the peaches are ripe, the seller will often let you taste one, free of charge, so that you can decide for yourself.

6. Wine

French wine is inseparable from French cuisine, and every dish pairs nicely with a corresponding Burgundy, Beaujolais, or equivalent. To enjoy a glass or two outside of a dining setting, head to Rue Montorgueil in the 2nd Arrondisement, which has the city's biggest and best concentration of wine bars.

7. Molecular Gastronomy

French chemist Hervé This first demonstrated molecular cuisine in 1992. He compared recipes with a series of chemical reactions and explained how different ingredients were transformed into food. This developed into a highly original cuisine that combines molecules using new cooking methods, often at extremely cold temperatures. Never dull, this type of cuisine is definitely an interesting experience.

Eclairs in all flavours

8. Croque Monsieur

The name 'croque monsieur' comes from the French words 'croque', which means to bite, and 'monsieur', meaning gentleman or mister. If you ask a local where to get the best *croque monsieur*, they will probably tell you that their mum or grandmother made the best ones at home. Failing that, there are plenty of restaurants in Paris that serve this dish as a lunch item.

9. Haute Cuisine
One of the best ways to enjoy haute cuisine in Paris's high-end restaurants is to opt for the chef's tasting menu (*dégustation*), which gets you a host of dishes in smaller-than-usual portions. Quite a few of the top-notch addresses serve fixed lunch menus that are significantly cheaper than the à la carte options – but their popularity means you'll need to book weeks in advance.

10. Escargot
Cliché though it may be, snails (*escargot*) are readily available in Parisian bistros and restaurants, and offer a delicious and fairly

---

ETIQUETTE

The French tend to sit down later than the British for dinner, and around 8:30–9pm is advisable. The dining table is sacrosanct in France, to the extent that visitors often report receiving dirty looks for walking around eating a sandwich; phones at the table are also more frowned upon than elsewhere.

Taking your children out to a restaurant should not be a problem, although you should check beforehand with the more upmarket places. French children are used to eating out from an early age, and are therefore generally well-behaved in restaurants.

A service charge of 12 to 15 percent is, by law, included in the price given at restaurants, bars and cafés, so in theory you don't have to tip. However, it is polite when paying for drinks to round up the total and to leave one to five euros after a meal, if you had good service.

A dish of the famous escargot

cheap way to have (for many people) a culinary adventure – molluscular, rather than molecular, cuisine, if you will.

Classic to Contemporary

The great cuisines of the world can be counted on one hand, and French cuisine is one of them. What the term implies is an established, coherent body of ingredients, techniques and dishes, which have all been developed, studied and perfected by masters of the art over many years.

This is not to say that French food isn't evolving. New flavours are integrated into the cooking all the time, albeit carefully. Curry, lime, peppers, coconut and lemongrass are all fairly common ingredients on gastronomic menus. Most dishes remain French at the core, but exotic nuances are certainly part of the high-end experience. In the

The iconic Art Deco La Coupole

middle ground, couscous is eaten almost as often as bœuf bourguignon, and sushi seems to be the city's favourite fast food.

Even in terms of technique, French cooking has modernised; sauces and pastries, for example, tend to be lighter than they were previously, and vegetables are more prevalent. Menus have been simplified and better aligned to contemporary appetites.

The advantage of this from a visitor's perspective is that the classic dishes we dream about can still be found in authentic form on French tables. If you want French onion soup, you can find it. If you order steak au poivre, out will come that desired slab of beef in a creamy, peppery sauce that spills across the plate towards your crispy pile of frites.

Another thing that makes French food extraordinary (and the bad French food, on a gracious day, forgivable) is the degree to which it is social. Even with the increased pace of modern life, the French still believe in sitting down and sharing meals in good company over a bottle of wine – so much so, indeed, that one of the most prominent fashions in recent years has been for canteen-style restaurants where diners rub up together on plain wooden benches seated at long communal tables. After all, food in France is much more than just sustenance.

Where to Eat

Bistros tend to serve simple, traditional dishes. The food quality varies from one to the next, unlike the menus, which are practically carbon copies of one another: potato and herring salad, duck confit, beef daube, chocolate mousse and tarte Tatin are a few of the classic dishes. Brasseries (the louder, brighter, Belle Epoque option) often offer similar fare, but also specialise in seafood – heaps of oysters, mussels, langoustines, lobsters and clams spinning past on waiters' dexterous palms – and Alsatian dishes such as choucroute.

Standard, everyday cafés usually serve sandwiches, notably the classic *croque-monsieur* (grilled ham and cheese) and a variety of salads. However, modern cafés – trendy, chic establishments that pack in fashionable crowds – serve full menus, typically of contemporary, cosmopolitan food with a Mediterranean bent, and often at prices to match full-blown restaurants.

Fine Dining

At the high end, Michelin-starred restaurants range from being gloriously old-fashioned, with truffle-studded foie gras terrines and venison in grand old sauces, to being acrobatically cutting-edge. One of the best ways to enjoy such restaurants is to opt for the chef's tasting menu (*dégustation*), which gets you a host of dishes in smaller-than-usual portions. Quite a few of the top-notch addresses serve fixed lunch menus that are significantly cheaper than the à la carte options – but their popularity means you'll need to book weeks in advance.

Les Cocottes serves its dishes in cast-iron pots, hence its name

Global Cuisine

If you get to the point where you think you might burst if you look at another plate of French food, take a break at one of the city's international restaurants. Paris is especially good for food from Morocco, Thailand, Vietnam and Japan. The greatest concentration of Chinese and Vietnamese restaurants is in the 5th and 13th *arrondissements* (roughly speaking, the Latin Quarter and southeast to the new Left Bank), and Japanese restaurants are numerous in parts of the 1st (especially on and around rue Ste-Anne). The best Moroccan restaurants are dotted across the capital, but the area around the Bastille is a good place to start. There is also excellent Lebanese food to be found in the 8th and 16th *arrondissements* (Madeleine, Grands Boulevards, Champs-Élysées and West).

To Help you Order

Do you have a table? **Avez-vous une table?**
The bill, please **L'addition, s'il vous plaît**
I would like … **J'aimerais…**

tea **du thé**	pepper **du poivre**
coffee **un café**	salad **de la salade**
milk **du lait**	soup **de la soupe**
sugar **du sucre**	fish **du poisson**
wine **du vin**	seafood **des fruits de mer**
beer **une bière**	meat **de la viande**
water **de l'eau**	very rare **bleu**
bread **du pain**	rare **saignant**
butter **du beurre**	medium-rare **rose**
cheese **du fromage**	medium **à point**
chips (fries) **des frites**	well done **bien cuit**
salt **du sel**	

Menu Reader

agneau lamb
ail garlic
bœuf beef
canard duck
champignons mushrooms
chou cabbage
choufleur cauliflower
crevettes roses/grises prawns/shrimps
dinde turkey
épinards spinach
escargots snails
fraises strawberries
framboises raspberries
haricots verts green beans
huîtres oysters
jambon ham
moules mussels
œufs eggs
oignons onions
petits pois peas
poire pear
pomme apple
pomme de terre potato
porc pork
poulet chicken
riz rice
saucisse sausage
saumon salmon
thon tuna

Places to Eat

We have used the following symbols to give an idea of the price for a three-course meal for one, including half a bottle of house wine, tax and service:

€€€€ = over 70 euros
€€€ = 50–70 euros
€€ = 25–50 euros
€ = under 25 euros

The Islands

Auberge de la Reine Blanche 30, rue Saint Louis en l'Ile, www.aubergedelareineblanche.fr. This long-established little restaurant creates a homely atmosphere with bistro-style chairs and tables and copper pans hanging from the wood-beamed ceiling. The regularly changing menu offers classics such as *soup à l'oignon, coq au vin and tarte tatin*. €€

The Right Bank

Louvre and Tuileries

Le Fumoir 6 rue de l'Amiral-de-Coligny, www.lefumoir.com. Open daily 11am–2am. Facing the Louvre, spacious, sophisticated Le Fumoir is renowned for shaking some of the best cocktails in town. It serves light pan-European cooking, such as poached cod with a warm salad of fennel, tomatoes and olives. €€€

Le Grand Véfour rue de Beaujolais, www.grand-vefour.com. Set under the arches of the Palais-Royal, this is one of the most beautiful restaurants in Paris. Le Grand Véfour opened its doors in 1784 and has fed the likes of Emperor Napoleon and writers Alphonse Lamartine and Victor Hugo. Today it serves haute cuisine in the hands of chef Guy Martin. €€€€

Café Marly Palais du Louvre, 93 rue de Rivoli, www.cafe-marly.com. Rest from your labours at the Louvre in the lavish Second Empire-style rooms facing the Pyramid, or on the attractive covered terrace. The food is modern European, the service sometimes a bit slow. €€€€

Le Meurice Alain Ducasse 228 Rue de Rivoli, www.alainducasse-meurice.com. Here, cooking has been elevated to an art form, by one of only two chefs in the world to hold 21 Michelin stars throughout his career (two of which are held by Le Meurice). Expect truffles in abundance and superb vegetables from Provence. Reserve well ahead. €€€€

The Grands Boulevards

Chartier 7 rue du Faubourg-Montmartre, www.bouillon-chartier.com. The ambience at this historic budget option is an experience in itself: Belle Epoque decor, snappy waiters, shared tables and plenty of bonhomie. €

Drouant 16-18 place Gaillon, 2e, www.drouant.com. Open daily for lunch and dinner, this literary institution (the headquarters of the Goncourt and Renaudot prizes since 1914) is run by famed chef, Antoine Westermann and serves traditional French fare with a modern twist. Excellent wine list. €€€

CoCo Palais Garnier, entrance on place Jacques Rouché, http://restaurant-coco.com. With its two-storey undulating glass front, extravagant interior with copper ceilings and, most of all, its location inside the Palais Garnier, this is one of the most spectacularly sited restaurants in Paris. Splash out on *filet de boeuf*, roasted veal, or slide up to the bar for one of the sumptuous cocktails. €€€

Café de la Paix 5 place de l'Opéra, www.cafedelapaix.fr. The prices are steep, but this is one of the city's most historic cafés (it opened in 1862), and it is convenient for the Palais Garnier opposite and the department stores on boulevard Haussmann. There is a family-friendly brunch on Sundays. €€€€

Willi's Wine Bar 13 rue des Petits-Champs, www.williswinebar.com. Open for lunch and dinner, Mon–Sat. In business for over thirty years, this classy establishment near the Palais Garnier is great for a full-blown meal à table or simply a glass of wine at its high oak bar. €€€

Beaubourg, Marais, Bastille and East

L'As du Fallafel 34 rue des Rosiers, tel: 01 48 87 63 60. The best *falafel* in Paris is a meal in itself. There are also *shawarma* sandwiches in pitta bread. Great location in the heart of the Marais. Dine in or take it to a nearby square or bench to enjoy. €

Brasserie Bofinger 5–7 rue de la Bastille, www.bofingerparis.com. Close to the Opéra Bastille, the huge (300-seater) Bofinger is the archetypal Belle Epoque brasserie, complete with lush red-and-gold decor. It is a great place in which to enjoy delicious oysters and seafood, and specialities from Alsace such as *choucroute*. €€€€

Chai 33 33 cour St-Emilion,; www.chai33.com. This restaurant is set in a light, airy former wine warehouse with a view of Bercy park. Choose your wine according to six styles, from light with a bite to rich and silky, with refreshing fusion food to match. Unpretentious *sommeliers* are on hand to help with wine choices. €€€

Le Chateaubriand 129 avenue Parmentier, 75011; www.lechateaubriand. net. This 'néo-bistrot' headed up by acclaimed chef, Iñaki Aizpitarte, has been awarded a Michelin star in the past and is consistently voted in the top 10 of best restaurants in the world. Daily changing menu. Book well in advance. €€€€

Chez Omar 47 rue de Bretagne, tel: 01 42 72 36 26. Couscous is one of the most popular international dishes in Paris, and this perennially popular address does some of the best. It doesn't take bookings, so you will have to get there early or join the queue outside. The portions are hearty, and the roast lamb is superb. €€

Chez Prune 36 rue Beaurepaire, tel: 01 42 41 30 47. This is a cornerstone of the trendy Canal St-Martin area, and a great spot from which to watch the world go by. Good food at lunchtime; tapas-style snacks at night. €€

Le Petit Fer à Cheval 30 rue Vieille-du-Temple, www.cafeine.com. Open for lunch and dinner daily. With its tiny horseshoe-shaped bar, this café on the Marais's trendy rue Vieille-du-Temple, is atmospheric and a great favourite with the bourgeois-bohemian crowd. Decent food. Friendly service. €€

Le Square Trousseau 1 rue Antoine-Vollon, www.squaretrousseau.com. A spacious bistro with Art Deco lamps, colourful tiles, a glamorous bar and terrace facing a leafy square. Among the delights available are gazpacho, tuna tartare, rosemary lamb and spring vegetables, beef with shallot sauce, and raspberry gratin. €€€

Le Train Bleu Gare de Lyon, www.le-train-bleu.com. Open for lunch and dinner daily. Built over a century ago, this huge restaurant in the Gare de Lyon is an artistic marvel, with frescoed ceilings and Belle Epoque murals. Classic French dishes are efficiently served. Good value set menus. There is also a bar. €€€€

Végét'Halles 41 rue des Bourdonnais, http://vegethalles.fr. Good-value vegetarian and vegan restaurant southeast of Les Halles. The menu includes salads, mushroom roast with blackberry and ginger sauce and there is a good choice of desserts such as fruit crumble or chocolate and banana cake. €€

Champs-Élysées and Trocadéro

L'Entredgeu 83 rue Laugier, www.lentredgeu.fr. Open for lunch and dinner Mon–Fri, dinner only on Sat. The unpronounceable name and non-central location apart, this superior bistro has a lot going for it. Dishes include roast duckling in honey sauce and lots of foie gras, and the decor is suitably cosy and intimate. **€€**

Le Pavillon Elysée Lenôtre 10 avenue des Champs-Élysées, 75008; www.lenotre.com. This pâtisserie is opposite the Grand Palais, in a glass pavilion created for the 1900 World Fair. The main reason to come here is for the delicious cakes, for which Lenôtre is best known. It's also possible to have a three-course meal. **€€€**

Western Paris

Pré Catelan Bois de Boulogne, https://leprecatelan.paris. This is one of the most romantic spots in Paris, situated in the heart of the Bois de Boulogne. Haute cuisine, centring on fresh truffles, lobster, lamb and fresh seafood. Book well ahead. **€€€€**

Montmartre and the Northeast

Le Coq Rico 98 rue Lepic, www.lecoq-fils.com. If you love poultry then this smart restaurant from Antoine Westermann is the place to come. Try the roast chicken accompanied by homemade chips, simple and delicious. **€€€€**

Rose Bakery 46 rue des Martyrs, www.rosebakery.fr. Considered a folly when it opened in 2002, this deli-style café run by a Franco-British couple quickly made its mark, and is still going strong. The ingredients are of the highest quality, and make the soups, salads and quiches really shine. Vegetarian options. **€€**

Chez Toinette 20 rue Germain-Pilon, http://cheztoinette.fr. With its red walls and romantic lighting, this cosy and convivial bistro in the heights of Montmartre is a good bet for a classic French dinner. Try the wild boar terrine, and don't miss the superb crème brûlée. €€€

The Left Bank

Latin Quarter and St-Germain-des-Prés

L'Alcazar 62 rue Mazarine, www.alcazar.fr. Sir Terence Conran's contribution to the Paris restaurant scene was to transform this former music hall into a designer brasserie. It's been a hit, thanks to the easy-going atmosphere and competitively priced menu, which includes an upmarket interpretation of British fish and chips. DJs play on the mezzanine Tue–Sat. €€€

L'Atelier de Joël Robuchon Hotel du Pont Royal, 5 rue Montalembert, http://atelier-robuchon-saint-germain.com. Parisians queue up in all weathers to sample the warm *brochettes de foie gras*, or tapenade with fresh tuna conjured by Axel Manes, the Michelin-starred protégé of France's most revered chef. The two-star Michelin restaurant is set around an open kitchen, so you can watch the masters at work. A second Atelier can be found at Publicis Drugstore (www.publicisdrugstore.com) on the Champs-Élysées featuring set lunch menus. Gluten-free menu is also available. €€€€

Le Comptoir Hôtel Le Relais St-Germain, 9 carrefour de l'Odéon, www.hotel-paris-relais-saint-germain.com. Open for lunch and dinner daily. Since its launch in 2005, chef Yves Camdeborde's Art Deco restaurant – in the 17th century hotel he runs with his wife Claudine – has been a steady hit with the city's gastronomes. Queues at lunchtime say all you need to know about the superb updated brasserie fare, such as chicken *basquaise* or salmon croque-monsieur. Tables are tightly packed, and the atmosphere is always convivial. You'll need to book ahead for the set menu dinner. €€€

La Ferrandaise 8 rue de Vaugirard, www.laferrandaise.com. Open for lunch and dinner Mon–Fri, dinner only Sat. An old-fashioned red entrance sets the tone for this Left Bank restaurant, with its three atmospheric dining rooms boasting exposed beams and tiled floors. The food is traditional French: try the sardines cooked in lemon juice or the succulent Bresse chicken with morel mushrooms. €€€

Guy Savoy Monnaie de Paris, 11 quai de Conti, www.guysavoy.com. Open for lunch Tue–Fri, Sat dinner only. The son of a gardener, Guy Savoy has an obsession with vegetables that has anticipated the current trend by more than a decade. The Michelin-starred chef happily pairs truffles with lentils or artichokes, and regularly makes the rounds to greet his guests. €€€€

Polidor 41 rue Monsieur-le-Prince, www.polidor.com. Open for lunch and dinner daily. This bohemian restaurant is a perennial favourite of students and budget diners. The *plats du jour* have been reliable for around 150 years and arrive in hearty helpings. *Bœuf bourguignon* and *tarte tatin* are just the kind of traditional dishes to expect here. €€

Le Rostand 6 place Edmond-Rostand, https://lerostand.fr. This is one of the city's more upmarket cafés, with prices to match – but it's the sort of place you should treat yourself to at least once on a trip to Paris. A fine view of the Jardin du Luxembourg, good cocktails, a delicious snacks menu and an attractive mirrors-and-mahogany interior make this a classy spot for refreshment. €€€

Around the Eiffel Tower

Au Bon Accueil 14 rue de Monttessuy, tel: 01 47 05 46 11. This elegant bistro serves modern classics. The *prix-fixe* dinner menu is viewed by many locals as one of the best deals in the neighbourhood, and the wine list is excellent. Seats on the terrace have views of its near neighbour the Eiffel Tower. €€€€

Les Cocottes 135 rue St-Dominique, http://lescocottes.paris. Open for lunch and dinner daily. This contemporary bistro run by chef Christian Constant has been packing Parisians in for its non-stop service of affordable and hearty grub: things like pumpkin soup or preserved shoulder of lamb. The name alludes to the cast-iron pots the food comes to the table in. €€€

Le Jules Verne 2nd floor, Eiffel Tower, www.restaurants-toureiffel.com. Location-wise, this restaurant on the second level of the Eiffel Tower is perfect for a celebration or romantic dinner, and it has received two Michelin stars for its high-end cuisine. Specialities include pan-seared turbot with yuzu and *beurre blanc*. €€€€

Montparnasse

La Closerie des Lilas 171 boulevard du Montparnasse, www.closeriedeslilas.fr. This historic brasserie still has a lot of charm and richly satisfying fare, though it lives off its reputation as a watering hole in the 1920s – tables are inscribed with the names of clients Lenin, Modigliani and André Breton. A pianist plays in the evening. €€€€

La Coupole 102 boulevard du Montparnasse, www.lacoupole-paris.com. Open for breakfast, lunch and dinner daily. Opened in 1927, this vast, iconic Art Deco brasserie, now run by the Flo Brasserie group, is still going strong. Brasserie fare includes huge platters of shellfish and grilled meats. €€€

Travel Essentials

Practical information

Accessible Travel	**129**
Accommodation	**129**
Airports	**130**
Apps	**131**
Bicycle Hire (Rental)	**131**
Budgeting for Your Trip	**131**
Camping	**132**
Car Hire (Rental)	**132**
Climate	**132**
Crime and Safety	**133**
Driving	**133**
Electricity	**134**
Embassies and Consulates	**134**
Emergencies	**134**
Getting There	**135**
Guides and Tours	**135**
Health and Medical Care	**135**
LGBTQ+ Travel	**136**
Lost Property	**136**
Money	**137**
Opening Hours	**137**
Police	**137**
Public Holidays	**138**
Telephones	**138**
Time Differences	**139**
Tipping	**139**
Toilets	**139**
Tourist Information	**139**
Transport	**140**
Visas and Entry Requirements	**141**
Websites	**141**

Accessible Travel

The Paris Tourist Bureau (http://parisjetaime.com) lists several companies (usually pharmacies) that rent wheelchairs and mobility scooters, such as Bastide le Confort Medical (39 rue Hermel, tel: 01 53 92 52 52; www.bastide leconfortmedical.com). **G7** (see page 141) is one of the few taxi companies to have a fleet of wheelchair accessible vehicles. Wheelchair users can visit http://parisjetaime.com/eng/practical-paris/visiting-paris-with-a-disability-i053 for guided tours tailored to disabled visitors.

Useful Organisations

France: Association des Paralysés de France, Service Information, 17 blvd Auguste Blanqui, 75013; tel 01 40 78 69 00; www.apf-francehandicap.org.
UK: Disability Rights UK, Plexal, 14 East Bay Lane, London E20 3BS; tel: 0330 995 0400; www.disabilityrightsuk.org.
US: Society for Accessible Travel and Hospitality (SATH), 347 Fifth Ave., Suite 605, New York, NY 10016; tel: 212 447 7284; www.sath.org.

Accommodation

Paris is a popular destination all year round, so booking in advance is always recommended, especially from May to September and during the two annual fashion weeks. Most hotels stay open in the quieter months, but booking ahead is still a good idea, as many establishments offer discounts or package deals.

For a long stay you might consider renting a serviced apartment; there are any number of homes available on **Airbnb** (www.airbnb.co.uk). Travel sections of national newspapers carry advertisements; the *International Herald Tribune* and Fusac (https://fusac.fr) list accommodation for rent.

Do you have a single/double room? **Avez-vous une chambre pour une/deux personnes?**
What's the rate per night? **Quel est le prix pour une nuit?**

Airports

Paris has two main international airports. **Roissy-Charles-de-Gaulle (CDG)**, 30km (19 miles) northeast, and **Orly (ORY)**, 18km (11 miles) south. For information on both, see www.parisaeroport.fr.

Charles-de-Gaulle to Central Paris

Train: The quickest way to central Paris from Roissy is by RER (line B) train. They leave roughly every 7–8 minutes from station Roissypole (for Terminal 1 and 3) and station CDG 2 (for Terminal 2) and run to the Métro stations at Gare du Nord and Châtelet, taking about 30 minutes. The Passe Navigo Découverte is valid. See http://parisbytrain.com for up-to-date info.

Bus: Roissybus (www.parisaeroport.fr) runs to rue Scribe (near the Palais Garnier) from terminals 1, 2A-2C, 2D-2B, 2E-2F and 3 (bus station). The journey time is 60 minutes. The five-zone Passe Navigo Découverte is valid. Alternatively, Le Bus Direct runs daily every 30 minutes from CDG 1 and 2: the green-coded line 2 runs to Av de Suffren, near the Eiffel Tower, stopping near the Champs-Elysées and at the Trocadéro on the way (1hr 10min to the Eiffel Tower), while the orange-coded line 4 stops at Gare de Lyon before terminating near Gare Montparnasse (1hr 15 min to Montparnasse). Magical Shuttle (http://magicalshuttle.co.uk) provides a direct service to Disneyland.

Taxi: Can take anything from 30 minutes to over an hour. Fares are metered, with supplements charged for each large piece of luggage; expect to pay in the region of €50–80.

Orly to Central Paris

Train: Take the local bus from gate F at Orly Sud or arrivals gate G at Orly Ouest to RER station Pont de Rungis (line C). Trains stop at St-Michel Notre-Dame and Champ de Mars Tour Eiffel, running every 15 minutes from 5am to 11.30pm. The journey takes around 30 minutes. Alternatively, take the Orlyval shuttle train from gate K at Orly Sud or departure gate A at Orly Ouest to RER station Antony (line B). Trains stop at St Michel Notre-Dame, Châtelet Les Halles and Gare du Nord. Orlyval services run every 7 minutes from 6am to 11.35pm; the RER runs every 15 minutes. Journey time

is about 30 minutes.
Bus: The Orlybus runs to Métro Denfert-Rochereau from Orly Sud gate G or Orly Ouest arrivals gate D. It runs every 10–20 minutes from 6am to 12.30am. The trip takes around 30 minutes; the four-zone RATP Navigo pass is valid.

The Bus Direct line 1 purple service runs daily from 6am–11.40pm, every 20 mins to Etoile/Champs Elysées, stopping at Gare Montparnasse, the Eiffel Tower and Trocadéro. The journey takes about 1hr to Etoile/Champs Elysées.
Taxi: The journey from Orly to the city centre takes 20–40 minutes.
Tram: Tramway 7 links the airport with Villejuif-Louis Aragon station (Metro line 7).

Apps
Bonjour RATP: The official public transport app, helping you plan journeys by bus, metro, RER, Transilien, and Tramway.
MisterGoodBeer: Your go-to guide for finding the best bars in Paris, with tips, table reservations, and discounts.
G7 Taxi: The local variation on the ubiquitous taxi-hailing app.

Bicycle Hire (Rental)
Cycling in Paris is easy thanks to the Vélib' scheme (www.velib-metropole.fr). Vélib' lets you pick up and return one of over 20,000 bikes (30 percent of which are electric) at any of 1,800 automated stations all over the city. A card valid for a week or a day can be bought from the stations, or online in advance. You then pay for each journey you make, according to its duration; trips under 30 minutes are free.

Alternatively, you can hire bikes and tandems by the day or week from Paris à Vélo C'est Sympa (22 rue Alphonse Bourdon, www.parisvelosympa.com); the company also operates guided cycle tours of the city.

Budgeting for Your Trip
The price of accommodation varies widely. You can get a double room in a small pension for under €100 a night, or you can pay over €500 in

a luxury hotel. An average price, however, for an en-suite double room in a centrally located, comfortable hotel is around €120–180. Meals also cover a wide price range, but on average expect to pay around €50–80 for a three-course meal with a half-bottle of house wine (though set menus cut costs). In everyday cafés and bars, a single espresso usually costs in the region from €3, and a pint of lager about €7. The average entrance price to a national museum or gallery is about €10–14 (municipal museums are free).

Camping

The only campsite within inner Paris (there are many more in the Paris region, for details see http://en.parisinfo.com) is Camping de Paris – Bois de Boulogne (2 allée du Bord de l'Eau, 75016; www.campingparis.fr), which is open all year. The site has cottages, wood trailers and canvas tents for hire as well as 35 pitches for guests with their own tents.

Car Hire (Rental)

To rent a car you will need your driver's licence and passport, as well as a major credit card or a large deposit. The minimum age for renting cars is 21, and you must have held a licence for at least a year. Third-party insurance is compulsory; full cover is recommended.

Among the international car-hire firms operating in Paris are:
Avis, www.avis.fr.
Budget, www.budget.com.
easyCar, www.easycar.com.
Europcar, www.europcar.com.
Hertz, www.hertz.com.

Climate

In winter temperatures in Paris average 4°C (39°F); in summer around 22°C (72°F). Spring and autumn tend to be mild, with an average of 11°C (52°F). June, September and October are ideal for visiting, as they are warm, usually sunny, but less stifling than midsummer.

Crime and Safety

Paris is a relatively safe city. There are pickpockets active in some Métro stations and at major tourist sites. Obvious centres of prostitution (such as rue St-Denis and parts of the Bois de Boulogne) are best avoided at night. It is always a good idea to keep a photocopy of your passport in case of theft. In the event of loss or theft, you'll need to make a report at the nearest police station (*commissariat de police*), which will be required if you wish to claim on your insurance.

Following the November 2015 attacks, expect extra security checks at airports and major attractions. Be aware that suitcases, travel bags and backpacks exceeding 55 x 35 x 25cm (21 x 14 x 10ins) will not be allowed in most museums and cannot be left at cloakrooms.

Driving

Driving in Paris requires both confidence and concentration. Traffic drives on the right, seat belts are obligatory, and the speed limit in town is 50kph (30mph). Do not drive in bus lanes at any time, and give priority to vehicles approaching from the right. This applies to some roundabouts, where cars on the roundabout stop for those coming on to it. Most car parks are underground (see www.parkingsdeparis.com), and street parking is hard to find; spaces are usually metered Mon–Sat 9am–8pm (payment can only be made with a Paris Carte, €15 or €30 from local tabacs or using the PaybyPhone app), and maximum stay is two hours. Fuel can be hard to find in the city centre, so if your tank is almost empty head for a *porte* (exit) on the Périphérique (the multi-lane ring road), where petrol stations are open 24 hours a day. The complete list of addresses can be found on the tourist office website (see page 139).

Drivers are liable to heavy on-the-spot fines for speeding and drink driving. The drink limit in France is 50mg/litre of alcohol in the blood (equivalent to about two glasses of wine), and is strictly enforced.

If you break down, contact Europ Assistance (tel: 01 41 85 85 85), but expect to pay a high cost unless you have already taken out its insurance cover.

> driver's licence **permis de conduire**
> car registration papers **carte grise**
> Yield to traffic from right **Priorité à droite**
> Slow down **Ralentir**
> Keep right/left **Serrez à droite/à gauche**
> One way **Sens unique**
> Give way **Cédez la priorité/le passage**

Electricity

You'll need an adapter: French sockets have two round holes. Supplies are 220 volt, and US equipment will need a transformer.

Embassies and Consulates

Australia 4 rue Jean-Rey, 75724; tel: 01 40 59 33 00; https://france.embassy.gov.au/pari/home.html
Republic of Ireland Embassy: 12 avenue Foch, 75116; tel: 01 44 17 67 00; www.ireland.ie/en/france/paris/
UK Embassy: 35 rue du Faubourg-St-Honoré, 75383; tel: 01 44 51 31 00; www.gov.uk/world/organisations/british-embassy-paris.
US Embassy: 2 avenue Gabriel, 75008; tel: 01 43 12 22 22; https://fr.usembassy.gov

Emergencies

Ambulance (SAMU) 15
Police (*police secours*) 17
Fire brigade (*sapeurs-pompiers*) 18
From a mobile phone: 112

> Fire! **Au feu!**
> Help! **Au secours!**

Getting There (see also Airports)

By Air: Air France is the main agent for flights to France from the US and within Europe and also handles bookings for some of the smaller operators, such as HOP!. For British travellers, operators such as British Airways (www.ba.com) and the low-cost airlines easyJet (www.easyjet.com), Flybe (www.flybe.com) and Jet2 (www.jet2.com) offer flights to Paris from London and other British cities. See www.skyscanner.net to compare prices.

By Rail: The Eurostar is the most convenient way to get to Paris (Gare du Nord) from the UK, with fast, frequent rail services from London (St Pancras International), Ebbsfleet and Ashford. The service runs about 12 times a day and takes two and a quarter hours (two hours from Ebbsfleet). For reservations, contact Eurostar on tel: 0343 218 6186 (UK) or 08 92 35 35 39 (France), or visit www.eurostar.com. There are reduced fares for children aged 4–11.

By Car: Eurotunnel takes cars and passengers from Folkestone to Calais on Le Shuttle. It takes 35 minutes from platform to platform and about one hour from motorway to motorway. You can book in advance with Eurotunnel on tel: 0844 879 7371 (UK) or 08 10 63 03 04 (France) or at www.eurotunnel.com or just turn up and take the next available service. Le Shuttle runs 24 hours a day, all year, and there are between two and five an hour.

By Bus: National Express subsidiary Eurolines runs daily services from London (Victoria Coach Station) to Paris (Métro Gallieni), providing one of the cheaper ways to get there. For more information, tel: 0871 781 81778 (UK) or 08 92 89 90 91 (France), or visit www.eurolines.eu.

Guides and Tours

Find multilingual guides and interpreters through the tourist office (see page 139). One of the best suppliers of guided tours is Paris Walks, which has been going for nearly 20 years; see www.paris-walks.com. To save shoe leather, try a tour on a Segway - see www.fattiretours.com for more details.

Health and Medical Care (see also Emergencies)

EU & UK Nationals: EU & UK nationals can receive emergency medical treatment. You will have to pay, but can claim from the French Sécurité

Sociale, which refunds up to 70 per cent of your medical bill. You must have a European Health Insurance Card (www.ehic.org.uk).

North American Citizens: Contact the International Association for Medical Assistance to Travellers (iamat), tel: 416 652 0137 (Canada) or 716 754 4883 (US), www.iamat.org. This non-profit group offers members fixed rates for medical treatment from participating physicians.

English-speaking health services are at the American Hospital, tel: 01 46 41 25 25, www.american-hospital.org, and the Hertford British Hospital, tel: 01 46 21 46 46, www.british-hospital.org.

Chemists: Pharmacies can be identified by their green (usually neon-lit) 'plus' sign. Pharmacie des Halles (10 boulevard de Sébastopol, Métro Châtelet; tel: 01 42 72 03 23) is open 8am–9pm, Mon-Sat. La Pharmacie de la Place de la République (5, place de la République, Métro République; tel: 0 1 47 00 18 08) is open 7 days a week, 24 hours a day.

LGBTQ+ Travel

The city has a large, visible and quite relaxed LGBTQ+ community. Gay bars and clubs are concentrated in the Marais. The magazine *Têtu*, available at kiosks, is a useful source of information (in French). For more information see the following websites in English: www.parismarais.com, www.gay-france.net and http://paris.gaycities.com.

Lost Property

If you lose your passport, report it to your consulate (see page 134).

If your credit card is lost or stolen, the numbers to ring are:

American Express, tel: +44 12 73 69 69 33
Mastercard, tel: +44 19 28 58 44 21
Visa, tel: 01 30 52 78 42 85

To reclaim anything else you have lost, you should go (with ID) to the Bureau des Objets Trouvés (36 rue des Morillons, Métro Convention; tel: 01 53 71 53 71; open Mon–Wed 8.30am–5pm, Thu 8.30am–noon, Fri 8.30am–4.30pm). You can contact them via their website (https://objetstrouves prefecturedepolice.franceobjetstrouves.fr) or by visiting the office in person.

Money

Currency: The euro (€) is divided into 100 cents (¢ or ct). Coins (*pièces*) come in 1, 2, 5, 10, 20 and 50 cents, and 1 and 2 euros. Banknotes *(billets)* come in 5, 10, 20, 50, 100, 200 and 500 euros. ATMs are widespread and accept most of the major international debit and credit cards; check withdrawal charges with your bank before you go.

Banks and currency exchange offices (banque; bureau de change): Take your passport when changing money or travellers' cheques. Your hotel may offer an exchange service, though at a worse rate.

Travellers' cheques: These are widely accepted (with identification).

> I want to change some pounds/dollars **Je voudrais changer des livres sterling/dollars**
> Do you accept travellers' cheques/this credit card? **Acceptez-vous les chèques de voyage/cette carte de crédit?**

Opening Hours

Traditionally, banks open Mon–Fri 9am–5pm and close at the weekend, though many now open on Saturday morning and close on Monday. Food shops tend to open early. Traditionally, most shops close for lunch, but in Paris, many remain open, closing at 7 or 7.30pm. The larger department stores do not close at lunchtime and are open until 9 or 10pm on Thursday. Most shops close on Sunday; many museums close on Monday or Tuesday and ticket offices usually shut at least 30 minutes prior to the official closing time.

Police (see also Emergencies)

The blue-uniformed police who keep law and order and direct traffic are, as a general rule, courteous and helpful to visitors. The CRS (*Compagnies républicaines de sécurité*) are the tough guys, brought in for demonstrations. The main police station is the Préfecture de Police, at 1 Rue de Lutèce (tel: 34 30).

If you need to call for police help, dial 17 (anywhere in France).

> Where is the nearest police station? **Où se trouve le commissariat de police le plus proche?**

Public Holidays
Public offices, banks and most shops close on public holidays, though you will find the odd corner shop open.

1 January *Jour de l'An* New Year's Day
1 May *Fête du Travail* Labour Day
8 May *Fête de la Victoire* Victory Day (1945)
14 July *Fête Nationale* Bastille Day
15 August *Assomption* Assumption
1 November *Toussaint* All Saints' Day
11 November *Armistice* Armistice Day (1918)
25 December *Noël* Christmas Day
Moveable dates:
Pâques Easter
Lundi de Pâques Easter Monday
Ascension Ascension Day
Lundi de Pentecôte Whit Monday

Telephones
Telephone numbers in France have 10 digits. Paris and Île de Fyrance numbers begin with 01; toll-free phone numbers begin with 0800; other numbers beginning with 08 are charged at variable rates; 06 numbers are mobile numbers.

UK mobile phones will work in Paris. For long stays, you can buy a pay-as-you-go (*sans abonnement*) mobile phone from Orange (www.orange.fr), SFR (www.sfr.fr), Bouygues Telecom (www.bouyguestelecom.fr) or Free (http://mobile.free.fr), all of whom have shops on French high streets.

Direct Dialling to Paris from the UK: 00 (international code) + 33 (France)

+ 1 (Paris) + an eight-figure number. To call abroad from France, dial the international access code (00), then the country code.
Directory Enquiries: 118 218, 32 12 (international enquiries).
Operator: 3123

Time Differences
France keeps to Central European Time (GMT +1 hour; GMT +2 hours Apr–Oct). When it is noon in Paris, it is 11am in London, 6am in New York, 10pm in Auckland, 8pm in Sydney and noon in Johannesburg.

> What time is it? **Quelle heure est-il?**

Tipping
By law, restaurant bills must include the service charge, usually 12 or 15 percent. Nevertheless, it is common to leave a small additional tip (around 5 percent) for the waiter, if the service has been good. With taxis, it is usual to round up to the nearest euro.

Toilets
There are automated public toilets (*sanisettes*) parked on pavements across the city; all are clearly marked. They are unisex, disinfected after each use, and free of charge. Most cafés have toilets, although these are, in principle, reserved for their customers.

Tourist Information
The main Paris tourism authority is the Office du Tourisme de Paris, http://parisjetaime.com. Branches are listed below.
Pyramides: 25 rue des Pyramides, 75001. Daily 9am–7pm (from 10am Nov–Apr). Gare du Nord: 18 rue de Dunkerque, 75010. Daily 8am–6pm. Gare de Lyon: 20 boulevard Diderot, 75012. Mon–Sat 8am–6pm. Gare de l'Est: place du 11 novembre 1918, 75010. Mon–Sat 8am–7pm. Anvers: 72 boulevard de Rochechouart, 75018. Daily 10am–6pm.

Transport

All public transport in Paris is run by the Régie Autonome des Transports Parisiens (RATP; tel: 32 46; www.ratp.fr). There is an information office at 54 quai de la Rapée, 75012 Paris.

Bus (*autobus*): Bus transport around Paris is efficient, though not always fast. You can obtain a bus route plan from Métro station ticket counters. Most buses run 7am–8.30pm, some until 12.30am. Service is reduced on Sundays and public holidays. Special Noctilien services operate on over 45 routes across the capital and suburbs, from 12.30am–5.30am every hour, with Châtelet as the hub.

Bus journeys take one ticket. You can buy a ticket as you board, but it is cheaper to buy a book of tickets (*carnet*) from any Métro station or tobacconist. Punch your ticket in the validating machine when you get on. You can also buy special one-, three- or five-day tourist passes or the weekly ticket and Navigo (see page 140). Show these special tickets to the driver as you get on, rather than putting them in the punching machine.

Métro: The Paris Métropolitain ('Métro') is fast, efficient and inexpensive. You get 10 journeys (including connections) for the price of seven with a *carnet* (book) of tickets. Tickets are also valid for the bus network and for the RER (in zones 1-2). Keep your ticket until you exit the station. A special ticket called **Paris Visite**, valid for one, three or five days, allows unlimited travel on the bus or Métro, and reductions on entrance fees to various attractions. A day ticket, **Mobilis**, is valid for the Métro, RER, buses, suburban trains and some airport buses. For longer stays, the best buy is a **Navigo** smart card, valid for unlimited rides inside Paris on the Métro and bus, either weekly (*hebdomadaire*) Mon–Sun, monthly (*mensuel*), or annual (*annuel*). Have a passport photo ready.

Métro stations have big, easy-to-read maps. Services start at 6am and finish around 1am (last trains leave end stations at 12.30am).

Train: The SNCF (French railway authority) is fast, comfortable and efficient. The **high-speed service** (TGV) is excellent but more expensive (www.sncf.com or www.voyages-sncf.com). Make sure you validate (*composter*) your train ticket before boarding by inserting it in one of the orange machines on the way to the platform.

Taxi: Taxis are generally reasonably priced, though there are extra charges for putting luggage in the boot and for pick-up at a station or airport. Taxi drivers can refuse to carry more than three passengers. The fourth, when admitted, pays a supplement.

You will find taxis cruising around or at stands all over the city, but finding an empty one can take a long time, especially at busy times of day. You can recognise an unoccupied cab by an illuminated sign on its roof. Fares differ according to the zones covered or the time of the day (you'll be charged more between 7pm and 7am and on Sunday). A fare between Roissy-Charles-de-Gaulle Airport and central Paris might be as much as €50 by day, €60 at night.

The following taxi companies take phone bookings 24 hours a day:
Alpha: 01 45 85 85 85; www.alphataxis.fr.
G7: 36 07; www.g7.fr. Also available as an app.

Visas and Entry Requirements

Nationals of EU countries need a valid passport or identity document to enter France. Nationals from Australia, Canada, New Zealand and the US need passports; South African nationals need a visa: visit https://fr-za.capago.eu for more information.

Websites

www.monuments-nationaux.fr Guide to national monuments
www.paris.fr General information on Paris from the city council
http://parisjetaime.com Paris official tourism site
www.parisvoice.com Online magazine about Paris for English speakers

Index

A
Académie Française 82
Arc de Triomphe 66
Arc de Triomphe du Carrousel 49
Arènes de Lutèce 79
Assemblée Nationale 86
Atelier Brancusi 58

B
Bagatelle 70
Banque de France 48
Bateau-Lavoir 73
Belleville 64
Bercy 63
Berthillon 42
Bibliothèque Nationale Richelieu 48

C
Cabarets 102
Centre National de la Photographie 19, 50
Centre Pompidou 56
Champ de Mars 88
Champs-Elysées 65
Cimetière de Montmartre 73
Cimetière du Montparnasse 92
Cinémathèque Française 63
Cité de la Musique - Philharmonie de Paris 75
Cité de l'Architecture et du Patrimoine 67
Cité des Sciences et de l'Industrie 74
Clubs and Bars 100
Conciergerie 40
courtyard 77

D
Disneyland Paris 97

E
Ecole Militaire 88
Eglise du Dôme 88

F
Fontainebleau 95
Fontaine des Innocents 58
Forum des Halles 58

G
Galerie des Glaces 94
Galerie des Rois 38
Giverny 97
Grande Arche 92
Grande Galerie de l'Evolution 80
Grand Palais 65
Grand Trianon 94

H
Hameau 95
Hôtel des Invalides 87
Hôtel de Soubise 59
Hôtel de Sully 61
Hôtel de Ville 56
Hôtel Lambert 43
Hôtel Lauzun 43

I
Ile St-Louis 42
Institut du Monde Arabe 80

J
Jardin d'Acclimatation 70
Jardin des Plantes 80
Jardin des Tuileries 49
Jardin du Luxembourg 83
Jazz, Pop and Rock 100
Jeu de Paume 50

K
Kiosque-Théâtre Madeleine 54

L
La Géode 75
La Machine 73
La Madeleine 53
Les Deux Magots, Café de Flore 81
Library du MAD 48
Louvre 44

M
Maison de Balzac 69
Malmaison 96
Marais 59
Marché aux Fleurs 42
Markets 105
Montmartre 71
Moulin Rouge 73
Musée Adam Mickiewicz 44
Musée Carnavalet 60

Musée Cernuschi 71
Musée Cognacq-Jay 60
Musée d'Art et d'Histoire du Judaïsme 62
Musée d'Art Moderne de la Ville de Paris 68
Musée de la Musique 75
Musée de l'Armée 87
Musée de l'Orangerie 19, 51
Musée des Arts Décoratifs 47
Musée des Arts et Métiers 19, 59
Musée d'Orsay 86
Musée du Louvre 45
Musée du Quai Branly 90
Musée Jacquemart-André 71
Musée Marmottan-Monet 69
Musée National d'Art Moderne 57
Musée National du Luxembourg 84
Musée National du Moyen Age 78
Musée National Eugène Delacroix 82
Musée National Picasso 60
Musée National Rodin 87
Musée Nissim de Camondo 70
museum 61
Muséum National d'Histoire Naturelle 80

N

north tower 39
Notre-Dame 36

O

Odéon Théâtre de l'Europe 84
Opera and Ballet 100
Opéra Bastille 62

P

Palais de Chaillot 67
Palais de Justice 40
Palais de la Cité 40
Palais de la Découverte 66
Palais de Tokyo 68
Palais du Luxembourg 84
Palais Garnier 53
Palais-Royal 48
Parc de la Villette 74
Participant Sports 107
Petit Palais 66
Petit Trianon 95
Pigalle 74
place Charles de Gaulle 66
place de la Bastille 62
place de la Concorde 51
place de la Contrescarpe 79
place de la Sorbonne 77
place des Vosges 61
place du Tertre 73
place St-Michel 76
Pont-Neuf 42
Pyramid 45

Q

Quatre Temps 93

R

rose window 38
Royal Chapel 94
rue Mouffetard 79

S

Sacré-Cœur 72
Sainte-Chapelle 41
Site de Création Contemporaine 68
Spectator Sports 107
square du Vert-Galant 42
State Apartments 94
St-Etienne-du-Mont 79
St-Eustache 58
St-Germain-des-Prés 80, 81
St-Julien-le-Pauvre 76
St-Louis-des-Invalides 88
St-Louis-en-l'Ile 43
St-Pierre-de-Montmartre 73
St-Séverin 76
St-Sulpice 83
synagogue 62

T

Theatre 99
Tour Eiffel 88
Tour Montparnasse 92

V

Vaux-le-Vicomte 96
Versailles 94
Viaduc des Arts 62

W

Walt Disney Studios Park 97
What to buy where 103

THE MINI ROUGH GUIDE TO PARIS

First Edition 2025

Editor: Kate Drynan
Author: Daniel Stables
Picture Manager: Tom Smyth
Cartography Update: Katie Bennett
Layout: Ankur Guha
Production Operations Manager: Katie Bennett
Publishing Technology Manager: Rebeka Davies
Head of Publishing: Sarah Clark
Photography Credits: All images Shutterstock except: Ilpo Musto/Apa Publications 63; iStock 23, 25, 49, 52, 53, 67, 72, 89, 96; Kevin Cummins/Apa Publications 46, 50, 68, 77, 78, 90; Ming Tang-Evans/Apa Publications 41, 54, 82, 85, 86, 116, 118; Public domain 20, 26; Sylvaine Poitau/Apa Publications 28
Cover Credits: Eiffel Tower viewed from Champ de Mars park **Jerome Labouyrie/Shutterstock**

Distribution

UK, Ireland and Europe: Apa Publications (UK) Ltd; mail@roughguides.com
United States and Canada: Two Rivers; ips@ingramcontent.com
Australia and New Zealand: Woodslane; info@woodslane.com.au
Worldwide: Apa Publications (UK) Ltd; mail@roughguides.com

Special Sales, Content Licensing and CoPublishing

Rough Guides can be purchased in bulk quantities at discounted prices. We can create special editions, personalized jackets and corporate imprints tailored to your needs. mail@roughguides.com

roughguides.com

EU Representative

LOGOS EUROPE, 9 rue Nicolas Poussin, 17000, LA ROCHELLE, France; Contact@logoseurope.eu; +33 (0) 667937378

Printed by Finidr in Czech Republic

ISBN: 9781835292228

This book was produced using **Typefi** automated publishing software.

A catalogue record for this book is available from the British Library

All Rights Reserved
© 2025 Apa Digital AG
License edition © Apa Publications Ltd UK

No part of this book may be reproduced, stored in a retrieval system, or transmitted in any form or by any means – electronic, mechanical, photocopying, recording, or otherwise – without prior written permission from Apa Publications.

Contact us

Every effort has been made to ensure that this publication is accurate, free from safety risks, and provides accurate information. However, changes and errors are inevitable. The publisher is not responsible for any resulting loss, inconvenience, injury or safety concerns arising from the use of this book. If you notice any errors, outdated information, or potential safety risks, please send your comments with the subject line "Rough Guide Mini Paris Update" to mail@roughguides.com.